T0209247

Remember
WHO YOU ARE

Remember WHO YOU ARE

How to Find Your Soul's Purpose
and Connect with Your Higher Self

SHWETA GANDHI

ARCHWAY
PUBLISHING

Archway Publishing books may be ordered through booksellers or by contacting:

Archway Publishing
1663 Liberty Drive
Bloomington, IN 47403
www.archwaypublishing.com
844-669-3957

Interior Image Credit: Naziya Khan
Instagram.com/nazkstudio

ISBN: 978-1-6657-3733-3 (sc)
ISBN: 978-1-6657-3734-0 (e)

Library of Congress Control Number: 2023900768

Print information available on the last page.

Archway Publishing rev. date: 03/30/2023

Contents

Dedicated to you. May the wisdom in these pages accelerate your spiritual growth and help you attain self-realization.

Foreword

The Universe is not without mystery, joy, and gratitude!

I am sure there are very intriguing energetic circumstances around how you found this book and that is part of the wonder we will explore as we connect to all the energies and paths leading to our Higher Self.

We all enter the awareness of our true energetic selves in the most astonishing ways. Sometimes, it can be confusing and chaotic. You are not alone!

If you find yourself holding this book and reading this page, you are most likely at a period of your life when you experienced an upheaval or a spiritual awakening and are looking to find clarity on your journey.

This book offers years of knowledge and support to those on their journey. I hope it aids you well as you find spiritual resonance and alignment to your path and true self.

Everyone is on a different and unique part of their path and what I loved so much about working through this book and exploring its pages was that it guided and supported me in ways they felt harmonic to my own visionary destiny.

We find ourselves existing and being present in a very radical time in the evolution of the human experience and this book offers the guidance I feel is so key at this stage of our spiritual transformation of humanity.

I challenge you to rise to the occasion. Explore your gifts, venture out and be bold!

Joey Wargachuk – Holistic Practitioner Trainer and Executive Member of the IPHM
www.wargachuk.com

Introduction

You are the Universe, and the Universe is within you. Our bodies are made of the same elements of life found in stars at the center of the Milky Way galaxy. Just the way a group of stars form a constellation, similarly, a group of souls form a spirit family. Like stars, souls link up together, creating an intricate web that stretches through eternity.

The biggest spiritual truth is that we are all infinitely connected to each other. We are all one big soul family; we originated from the same Source and we will return to it. Due to the illusion of separation, we look different and speak differently, but our hearts are speaking the same language—love.

Right now, the world is going through *Kali Yuga*, the age of darkness, destruction, and conflict. Political structures are falling apart, economies are collapsing and countries are at war. COVID-19 is just another addition to the long list of problems humanity is facing as a collective.

All this is a huge wake-up call from Mother Earth to spiritually awaken and realize that we are eternal souls having a human experience in a beautifully-designed body that is only going to live for a limited number of years. Your aim is to utilize this precious time to work on your soul's purpose or mission for this life.

Following your Earthly passions or your soul's destiny is bound to bring you love, joy, and peace. These emotions emit high vibrations that transmit feel-good frequencies in the Universe which echo back to you.

To raise your vibration, you must become self-aware and conscious of your thoughts. Practicing mindfulness helps you observe your actions and emotions at every moment without judgment.

Enlightenment is the highest vibration of 700 Hz on Earth as well as in the heavenly realms. In this state, you are simply being. Everything just is. Nothing is amiss. It just *is*.

When you become aware of what is, your focus shifts to the good things in life. You begin to imbibe positive virtues which raise your soul's vibrational resonance.

From this enlightened state of mind, I invite you to begin a personal journey with your Higher Self where you explore the depths of your soul.

Why are you here?
What is your soul's purpose?
How do you intend on making this life count?

This book explores these questions and offers you guidance on how to live a meaningful life aligned with your soul's purpose. Each chapter explores a different theme and comes with a list of reflective questions. To maximize the benefits of this self-help book, take your time in answering the questions as your breakthroughs or sudden realizations will happen through them.

I sincerely hope this book enriches your spiritual journey and motivates you to live in accordance with your Higher Self.

Remember that enlightenment is always here and now. Life is an ongoing journey and every present moment holds the secret to happiness. Now, I am going to share that secret with you. Are you ready?

It's Time to Awaken

You are a soul here on planet Earth,
Having taken rebirth,
To share your light and positivity.

The darker souls will try to steal what they lack,
The love, the laughter, the optimism,
Because all they see is black.

Don't give in to the immoral souls,
Protect yourself from the darkness they hold,
See the shining light, white and gold,
Immerse yourself in consciousness only you know.

Be safe and be strong,
Be courageous and keep moving along.
In the end, it's only between you and God.

Part 1

Chapter 1

· · ❖ · ·

DECODING YOUR SOUL'S UNIQUE BLUEPRINT

Picture this: You and I are sitting in a huge classroom along with a group of students. We are all learning lessons and improving our skills in a variety of subjects. Each student has a project to work on. Our teacher, however, is invisible.

We learned the rules and the laws of this school millions of years ago, but we forgot and ended up failing our lessons. To make up for it, we kept coming back to the classroom to learn and grow. To create a fair and just learning system for all, the principal of this school ensured every student attending does not remember their past thoughts and actions.

This school your soul is attending is planet Earth. When you were born on Earth, you entered a state of amnesia wherein you forgot your past lessons and your soul's origins.

All souls originated from the Source of light, a heavenly realm of unmanifest potentiality and infinite possibilities where everything exists all at once. Time ceases to exist; all past and future timelines merge into the here and now. All souls are androgynous with both feminine and masculine qualities. Just like the creator, each soul can create through the power of its mind.

Why are we attending this Earthly school? To learn and grow. The initial idea to incarnate was to embody the qualities of our principal, the creator of this planet, and become more God-like.

It is now time to re-remember your real identity. You are not this body. You are not your mind. You are a soul inhabiting a physical vessel, here to serve society with your soul's gifts.

When you finally learn your lessons, your soul will attain *moksha* or liberation, and you will break free from the cycle of karma to progress further in your spiritual journey.

The world's oldest living religion, Hinduism, teaches that a human being's inherent nature is not limited to the body or the mind. Beyond this is the divine essence (or *Atman*, the soul) that lives within all beings and things. This *Atman* is eternal, infinite, and always united with its creator (or *Brahma*, the Universe, the ultimate reality). *Atman* is *Brahma*—our soul is the same as the Universe. This message reflects in Hermeticism as well, especially in the Law of Correspondence which states: "As above, so below. As within, so without. As the Universe, so the soul."

Atman, or the soul, cannot be destroyed; it has always existed and will continue to do so. The soul goes through continual cycles of rebirth wherein it enters a new human body in a different setting on Earth. The actions or karma a soul enacted in its previous lifetimes are what it reaps in its current existence. That is why some of us are born in fortunate circumstances and some of us live a rather difficult life.

Before a soul incarnates on planet Earth, it lays out a path, better known as a soul plan. This plan explores life lessons—the ideals of unconditional love, compassion, honesty, humility, righteousness, patience, tolerance, power, and self-control—that the soul attempts to master, and it is up to the soul to choose how easy or difficult they want their challenges in life to be.

Each soul's journey on Earth is guided by their Higher Self. This plan is a continuation of the soul's journey through consciousness. The storyline could vastly differ from the plan it created for itself in a previous life, or it could be in the same vein. In each life, the soul sets challenges to endure and overcome, with growth as the goal. However, the trials could differ dependent on the soul's age.

An infant soul, who has just begun its cycle of reincarnation, may choose simple lessons to navigate life on Earth.

A baby soul, still growing and learning, will pick up its easy lessons from where it left off.

A young soul, having lived a few hundred lives, could have accumulated karmic debt with its soul mates that it now strives to settle as it learns challenging life lessons.

A mature soul, having mastered some lessons and grown wiser through its reincarnations, may still choose to set itself up for tough tests.

An old soul, who has lived through thousands of lifetimes, may decide to incarnate to spread virtues of compassion and universal love to help raise the vibrations of its soul family.

A transcendental soul, who has settled its karmic debts and learnt all necessary lessons, could design a life where it aims to serve society through spiritual wisdom.

Then there are ascended masters like Buddha and Jesus who incarnate to school the masses and lead Earthlings toward the path of enlightenment.

*We are beings of light. We originated from light and we
will go back to light after this Earthly lifetime.*

Dependent on past lives and the learnings gleaned from them, each soul maps out a journey for its next life where it aims to maximize its strengths and work on its weaknesses. For example, a selfless mother who has devoted her life to caring for her family and tending to their needs must learn the importance of self-care, putting herself first, and standing up for herself. A mature soul who needs to master the lesson of perseverance could opt for a gruelling career that demands arduous amounts of hard work that constantly tests the soul's resilience. This creates a unique blueprint for each soul, ensuring that no two souls are identical, just the way no two soul plans are one hundred percent alike.

Every soul holds valuable and varied experiences—unbeknownst to the conscious mind—that give it a distinct way of looking at life. Each one of us has gifts to share; a certain uniqueness or a valuable skill that sets us apart from everybody else. To begin decoding your soul's purpose, it is important to realize your strengths. The journal prompts below will get you started.

EXERCISE 1: ACKNOWLEDGING YOUR STRENGTHS

Before starting this exercise, it is important to ground yourself with a lightwork meditation to relax your mind and become fully present. This will help your conscious mind settle down and allow your subconscious mind to open and express itself without judgment.

Sit in a comfortable position, and when you feel ready, close your eyes, and take a deep breath.
Inhale, exhale.
Envision white light surrounding your body. This healing light is warm and comfortable, and it soothes your worries and anxieties. Surrender your stress to this white light. Focus on this restorative feeling for one full minute. Upon opening your eyes, write down the first thoughts that come to you.

What skills come naturally to you?

_____

_____

_____

_____

_____

_____

What interests are you subconsciously drawn towards?

_____

_____

_____

_____

_____

_____

What are your creative hobbies?

_____

_____

_____

_____

_____

_____

If you could do one thing for the rest of your life and be paid for it, what would it be?

_____

_____

_____

_____

_____

_____

Note that there are no right or wrong answers—it all depends on how aware and aligned you are with your subconscious mind. The purpose of this exercise is to get you warmed up to the idea that change is possible, and that life is meant to be lived with meaning.

If you notice that your answers are repetitive, this is a sign that you are on the right track. You are aware of your soul's strengths.

If you are having trouble forming your thoughts and framing your answers, it is your conscious mind's resistance acting up. Practice the lightwork meditation once more and attempt writing again without your inner critic judging you.

The qualities or skills that you believe are your strong points are, in fact, your gifts. These gifts are unique, and you must utilize them to serve or give back to society. If you do that, you take a step in the right direction to fulfill your soul's purpose.

Now that you have shed light on your soul's strengths, it's time to look at the qualities you need to develop.

EXERCISE 2: ACCEPTING YOUR LIMITATIONS

Before you begin writing, ground yourself by visualizing a bright white light surrounding your body. This powerful healing light cleanses and refreshes you completely.

Now, write down the first thoughts that come to you.

What are some challenging areas of your life?

_____

_____

_____

_____

_____

_____

What are you most ashamed about?

_____

_____

_____

_____

_____

_____

What areas of your life could be better than they currently are?

_____

_____

_____

_____

_____

What do you dislike about yourself?

_____

_____

_____

_____

_____

_____

What dark qualities about yourself would you never share with anyone?

_____

_____

_____

_____

_____

_____

These questions may be difficult to answer, and you might even find this whole process ridiculous, but asking yourself such deeply penetrating questions can help lift the ego's veil to reveal your shadow self, the side you repress and hide from others.

Again, note that there are no right or wrong answers. Our darkest side is buried deep within layers of conditioning. Sometimes, scraping the surface can be painful enough. So, take your time and be gentle with yourself during this healing process.

The point of these exercises is to increase your level of self-awareness. The better you know yourself, the deeper the relationship will be with your Higher Self.

Now that you are aware of your soul's strengths and the challenges you must overcome, let's look at your life's ultimate purpose.

EXERCISE 3: RECOGNIZING YOUR HEART'S TRUE DESIRE

Before you begin writing, ground yourself by visualizing a bright white light surrounding your body. This powerful healing light cleanses and refreshes you completely.

Now, write down the first thoughts that come to you.

What do you really want to do in life?

_____

_____

_____

_____

_____

_____

What are your biggest goals and your most cherished dreams?

_____

_____

_____

_____

_____

_____

What pulls at your heartstrings and calls out to you the most?

_____

_____

_____

_____

_____

_____

What is a dream that keeps you up at night?

_____

_____

_____

_____

_____

Was it easier to answer this time around? Are you satisfied with the results?
Stay patient during this process of chipping away at old mental programs that
have been unconsciously running in your mind.

Once you have completed the exercises, read your notes again. Give yourself
time to fully absorb the answers. Sit with these messages for some time and
reflect on the guidance your Higher Self has given you.

Now that you have shed light on your unique gifts and the challenges that
your soul has chosen to navigate, it is time to gain more perspective on the
spiritual map of your life.

Chapter 2

・・❖・・

EXPLORING YOUR PRESENT LIFE'S STORY

When a soul decides to reincarnate or be reborn, it picks out a birth family that will best help it learn its lessons for that lifetime. The personality of the mother and the father plays a very important role in shaping a soul's life, especially during childhood.

A child learns to mimic the behavioural traits of his/her parents and siblings, and at an innocent young age, cannot differentiate between right and wrong. They don't think there would be any consequences to their actions or even their thoughts. Yet, children are the most carefree and innocent souls whose subconscious mind is wide awake. Kids between the ages of two and five are reportedly more likely to remember memories from their past lives. Some children have even been able to recall exact names and addresses, proving reincarnation is real[1].

Growing up, the soul will often look back at its childhood as many of its traumas, wounds, and emotional pain resides there. An inattentive parent,

---

[1] See the list of recommended readings at the end of this book for detailed reports of cases of reincarnation.

a bully at school, a critical teacher, or a mean friend could have caused long-lasting hurt or harm that the adult body remembers. Any embarrassing, painful, shameful, or fearful memories from your childhood are stored in your emotional body. Forgiving those who hurt or harmed you releases negative memories, blockages, and attachments.

Your story is your personal journey that is as unique as your soul's blueprint. Starting from your name to your date and time of birth, every aspect of your life is chosen by your soul before you were born on Earth.

This thought can seem daunting. If we chose our parents, our name, the day, the time we would be born, and the country as well, wouldn't we at least remember it? What's more, wouldn't it be convenient and advantageous for us to remember why we were born on Earth?

The answer is not so simple. This amnesia or partial memory loss of our true nature plays a pivotal part in our soul's plan. It gives everyone a fair chance to excel at their journey, and to explore their deepest motivations. Not knowing why you are here and what you are here to do kick-starts your spiritual journey as you set out to discover the answers to life's existential questions. By diving deep into mindfulness, you begin to remember who you are.

Relying upon traditional studies like Numerology (the study of numbers), Astrology (the study of planets and their movement), palmistry (the study of the palm), and face reading (the study of the face) can help reveal hidden aspects of your personality in this life. We will explore Numerology and Astrology in further detail in chapter 3.

My first ever instance of re-remembering age-old knowledge occurred when I was 16 years old. My mother's friend lent me her copy of *Many Lives, Many Masters* by Dr. Brian Weiss. Based on a true story, psychotherapist Dr. Weiss was shocked when his patient started recalling past-life traumas that were seemingly the root cause of her nightmares and anxiety attacks in this life. Apart from reinstating Hinduism's teachings on reincarnation, the book affirmed that past wounds can heal through regression therapy and that past-life karma could transmute if the soul decided to take the right actions in this life.

This was the first time I came across the idea of reincarnation and past lives, and my conscious mind did not reject it at all. It felt like I was re-learning concepts I already knew from before, just like how we would revise everything we have learned one last time before we sat for an exam. This profound insight into my deep well of stored knowledge and wisdom struck a chord with me.

A small but powerful realization occurred: the world or the external reality as we know it is not what it seems at face value. There exist other worlds and parallel Universes that are beyond our comprehension. The fact that our human brain cannot even begin to fathom those existences is what brings us to a vibration of fear and skepticism where we dismiss these ideas altogether.

The human race has been conditioned to believe in only what the eyes see. But what if the creator limited our ability to see and perceive everything? We are taught to reject ideas our mind cannot understand or scientifically prove. By doing this, we unknowingly limit our potential. General close-mindedness and a denial of spirituality are a deterrent to our soul's growth. We will grow regardless if we abide by the laws of the spiritual realm, but our growth will be slower as compared to a soul that is conscious of its true nature.

Reading spiritual texts and literature is the first step you can take to remember who you are and why you are here. Intellectual knowledge of the world's workings is accumulated first, and as you keep testing out your theories and learnings, you grow confident that you are indeed here for a reason.

You start believing in your Higher Self and develop faith in the process. You recognize that your soul chose to come down to planet Earth to live with purpose and passion. The ability to discern your Real Self from the *maya* or the façade of the physical world begins to take place, bringing about a profound spiritual awakening. Sometimes, you could inadvertently be jolted into a spiritual awakening through a disease or chronic sickness, a near-death experience, the loss of a family member/friend, deep meditation, fasting for long periods, or even a powerful adrenaline rush experienced through adventure sports.

As a result of your spiritual awakening, you could experience traumatic and triggering events in your life that test your limits and challenge your beliefs. Oftentimes, it feels like your whole life is falling apart and nothing seems to be going in your favour. Dark nights of the soul occur, wherein you question reality and yourself while experiencing bouts of anxiety, paranoia, and depression. Know that this is a sign of your ascension. Whatever is not serving your higher purpose anymore is breaking away, making room for bigger and better experiences in your life.

EXERCISE 4: ASSESSING WHERE YOU ARE IN YOUR JOURNEY RIGHT NOW

Where are you in your life's path today? The following journal prompts will get you to look deeper at your life's story.

Your full name, as on your birth certificate:

_____

Your date and time of birth, as on your birth certificate:

_____

Your place of birth:

_____

You identify as a:

_____

What is/was your relationship with your parents like?

_____

_____

_____

_____

_____

_____

What are you currently doing? (Studying/working—describe every detail.)

_____

_____

_____

_____

_____

_____

What would you like to do after this?

_____

_____

_____

_____

_____

_____

If you had additional resources (time/money), what would you be doing?

_____

_____

_____

_____

_____

What actions can you take right now to align yourself with your soul's purpose?

_____

_____

_____

_____

_____

_____

EXERCISE 5: CELEBRATING YOUR PAST

You will have life-altering moments that shaped you into who you are today. For example, the death of my grandfather affected me deeply as a 13-year-old. Reluctant to accept reality, I closed myself off from my classmates in school and withdrew into a shell. At home, I pretended to be unperturbed. The inability to express my inner emotional state to people made me turn to write my deepest feelings on a piece of paper. To date, whenever I feel sad, I journal about the incident in my diary. It is therapeutic and makes me feel lighter.

The passing of a loved one could be a moment that changed you, too. Or witnessing the birth of a child brought about a moment of transformation in your life. Perhaps it was the day you suffered a personal tragedy. Whether it is through loss, pain, suffering, or a miraculous divine intervention that awakened you, the onus is on you to recognize those moments when something shifted within you, and you became more of your Real Self.

What are some moments that shaped your life and made you who you are today?

_____

_____

_____

_____

_____

_____

What is one defining moment in your life so far?

_____

_____

_____

_____

_____

_____

What are your biggest regrets?

_____

_____

_____

_____

_____

If you could time travel to the past, what would you do?

_____

_____

_____

_____

_____

What actions can you take in this present moment to alleviate any past disappointments?

_____

_____

_____

_____

_____

List a few past achievements you are proud of.

_____

_____

_____

_____

_____

_____

_____

Chapter 3

•• ❖ ••

UNDERSTANDING YOUR PERSONALITY USING NUMEROLOGY AND ASTROLOGY

Numerical repetition and synchronicity have played a huge role in life on Earth for many years. Today, the teachings of the ancient Greek philosopher and mathematician Pythagoras who lived about 580 B.C. are the most common, termed as Modern Numerology.

Pythagoras believed that the material world was a composition of numbers that energetically vibrated at different frequencies. His quotes, "All things are numbers" and "God built the Universe on numbers," still ring true today. He devised a system wherein letters corresponded with integers, and this ancient system of Numerology used Hebrew glyphs to provide insights into our personality traits, karmic patterns, lessons, innermost desires, soul talents, and life goals.

One of his main teachings is that life is subject to predictable cycles that can be measured through numbers. As an initiate into the highest mysteries of Egypt and Asia, Pythagoras was privy to a mathematical formula that revealed the secrets behind the creation of the world.

This sacred formula is 10-5-6-5.

Translated into Hebrew, it makes up the Tetragrammaton Jod-Heh-Vau-Heh or JHVH, which means "name of the Lord" in the Hebrew Bible, and is one of the seven names of God in Judaism. Interestingly, the transliteration of Jod-Heh-Vau-Heh into Hindi roughly equates to "जो है वो है" or "Jo Hai Woh Hai" in Hinglish (a portmanteau of Hindi and English), which can be better understood in English as, "It is what it is" or "As is, so is". This profound secret of the Universe is also revealed in the Law of Correspondence ("As above, so below. As within, so without. As the Universe, so the soul.") in Hermeticism that we touched upon in Chapter 1.

Another note-worthy Italian mathematician, Leonardo Pisano Fibonacci, is known for his famous Fibonacci Series. Each number is the sum of the two preceding numbers: 0,1,1,2,3,5,8,13,21,34,55,89,144...

This Fibonacci sequence is mathematically proven by nature and is seen in the pattern of branches, spiralling patterns of leaves and flowers like daisies, patterns in fruits and vegetables such as pineapple and cauliflower, as well as in populations of rabbits and honeybees. This sequence is the rational progression towards the irrational number in the Golden Ratio/Phi Ratio/Golden Mean/Divine Proportion which is about 1.61803...

According to the Golden Ratio, the ratio of the whole to the larger section is the same as the ratio of the larger section to the smaller section. This offers an aesthetically-pleasing proportion, with the best visual example being the Great Pyramid of Giza whose construction was based on the Phi Ratio as the apothem to the bisected base ratio. Artist Leonardo da Vinci also famously used the Golden Ratio in his painting, *The Last Supper*.

This mathematical perfection of repetitive and predictable patterns displays a fundamental essence following an unfaltering geometrical design that is precise. This reinforces the idea that numbers reflect the underlying construction of the Universe.

The pyramids of Giza, located in Greater Cairo,
Egypt, were constructed using the Golden Ratio/Divine Proportion.

In the table below, explore the deeper meanings of the odd number (0) and the natural numbers (1-9) that form the original blueprint of all of life. Each number doubled, tripled, or quadrupled, like 11, 111, 1111, 22, 222, 2222, 33, 333, 3333…. and so on denotes a magnified amplitude of the number's qualities or personalities. Also known as Angel Numbers, seeing repetitive number patterns like these are a sign of your spiritual awakening with a divine message from the Universe. Ahead, let's decode the spiritual meanings of each number.

Numbers	Spiritual Meanings
0, 00, 000, 0000	Nothingness, nobody, formless, indescribable, divinity, everything exists and recycles endlessly
1, 11, 111, 1111	Action, individuality, self-awareness, self-expression, new beginnings
2, 22, 222, 2222	Duality, polarity, equal and opposite reaction, collection, assimilation, partnership

3, 33, 333, 3333	Expansion, unity, cooperation, growth, creativity, communication, holy trinity
4, 44, 444, 4444	Formation, order, measurement, matter, four elements, four seasons, four moon phases
5, 55, 555, 5555	Change, versatility, freedom to choose, independence, decision-making, critical thinking, development of conscious thought
6, 66, 666, 6666	The balance of opposites, harmony, social responsibilities, peace-loving, beauty, truth, justice
7, 77, 777, 7777	Success, rest, rainbow colours, spiritual seeking, secret keeper, messages from the spirit realm
8, 88, 888, 8888	Manifestation, energized positive thinking, cube, unending cycle, infinity, immortality
9, 99, 999, 9999	Completion, fulfillment, attainment, enlightenment, all-encompassing, nine lives of cats, practical wisdom, letting go of the material, donating money

Figure 1.1 The spiritual meanings of numbers.

EXERCISE 6: DECODING YOUR LIFE PATH USING NUMEROLOGY

If you study numbers, you will understand your real nature.

In this exercise, we will calculate the main number in Pythagorean Numerology: The Life Path number. This number is like your Astrological sun sign and describes the path your life will take for you to learn your karmic lessons. It also identifies your personality traits, strengths, weaknesses, talents, and ambitions.

The basic tenets of Numerology say that when you were born (time, day, date, month, and year) and the exact geographical location (longitude and latitude) plays a huge role in shaping your present life's destiny. It affects the journey your soul undertakes and defines your personality in many ways. Add the placements of the planets along with this information and you have your Astrological natal chart.

There are no coincidences on Earth. Our soul chooses when and where to be born. When I checked my birth certificate, I was shocked to discover that I was born at 3:33 am. I knew this was not by chance; it was a meaningful synchronicity meant to awaken my soul. The number 3 represents creativity and communication, and it is no wonder that my career revolves around fashion and lifestyle journalism, digital copywriting, and social media marketing.

Once you have determined your Life Path number, you can then read what it says about you and your life.

HOW TO CALCULATE YOUR LIFE PATH NUMBER

Your Life Path number is the sum of your date of birth.

Example: March 10, 1993
First, we add the month and the date: 3 + 10 = 13
Then, we add the year: 1 + 9 + 9 + 3 = 22
Now, we add both numbers: 13 + 22 = 35
3 + 5 = 8
Hence, 8 is the Life Path number.

The only rule is that all double digits (except the powerful master numbers 11, 22, and 33) are added again until we are left with a single digit.

Now, calculate your Life Path number.

_____

_____

_____

_____

Refer to the meaning of your Life Path number below to understand your personality's strengths and the possible roadblocks you could face.

Life Path Number 1
1 represents the beginning, the start of something new. You have a strong desire and need to create a positive impact on the world. You will strive to

create change through creative, artistic, innovative, and bold techniques that people around will love seeing and following. Your powerful demeanour comes across as original, and you highlight a healthy ego.

People will look up to you as a leader and a guide, but pay close attention so that you are not distracted by people pleasing. This could make you dependent on others, which could result in situations not in alignment with your soul's higher purpose. You need to remember what your values are, so you can stay true to yourself and lead with integrity.

Life Path Number 2

2 represents duality. You have a balanced approach to life, and you give equal importance to your external as well as your internal life. You are sensitive and genuine, and you practice honesty in all your endeavours. However, you could be prone to indecision, or your moods could oscillate from extreme happiness to abject despair. When faced with difficulties or harsh criticism, you could give in to fear, and the habit of overthinking could get you stuck in a negative spiral.

You need to imbibe a positive frame of mind that allows you to find the unseen benefit during dark nights of the soul. Try to work out where your inner critic comes from and release self-defeating beliefs by acknowledging and accepting them. You could also benefit from physical exercise that will fight off the lethargy you are likely to face.

Life Path Number 3

3 represents creativity and communication. You have a magnetic personality and you are likely to be part of large social circles. Your optimistic frame of mind attracts all sorts of people vibrating at different levels.

You could be tested by temptations that could distract you from your journey. A non-committal attitude to life could result in half-finished projects and a little bit of energy devoted to a wide range of goals. It is your responsibility to discipline yourself in all endeavours, and practice saying no to people, places, or circumstances that do not align with your Higher Self's vision. How do you know what is best for you? Ask a question and then tune in to your heart to see how you feel. Your feelings will guide you to the right answer.

Life Path Number 4

4 represents formation and order. You are blessed with strong willpower and a practical personality that allows you to tread the path of perseverance and hard work. You are clear about what you want and you know what you must do to achieve those desired results. You have faith in your abilities and you follow the plan you set out.

However, you can be very rigid in your approach to life situations and could end up stagnating. Your innate need to control situations can lead to disappointment when things do not go as planned. You could also have difficulties trusting others. You need to learn to surrender your control and allow more freedom and flexibility in your plans.

Life Path Number 5

5 represents change and independence. You are an open-minded, flexible thinker who can find solutions outside the box. You are a grounded person who stays anchored in the present moment because you understand the temporary nature of time.

The shadow side of this aspect could manifest as self-indulgence and an attraction to sense pleasures that are transient in nature. You could resist change, and this could backfire on your efforts to reform. You could also be too focused on your life, neglecting your family and friends' needs. Try adopting a positive attitude towards people to attract positivity in your own life.

Life Path Number 6

6 represents balance and harmony. You are a compassionate and magnanimous soul; you radiate positivity wherever you go. You are full of love and you enjoy nurturing everyone from kids to animals to your family members. People in your life look up to you and respect you for the goodness you selflessly shower. The love you receive gives you emotional fulfillment.

The other side of this aspect is that you could get caught up in giving of yourself that you burn out physically, emotionally, and mentally. You need temperance. This will help you find time to do things you love and practice self-care. Know that your value is greater than what you can offer to others and learn to draw boundaries between yourself and people.

Life Path Number 7

7 represents spirituality and success. You are a peaceful and reflective being who enjoys slow living. Spending time in nature recharges you. You enjoy connecting with others but you don't let their thoughts and opinions define your life. Your balanced approach to life brings about harmonious relationships.

However, you could struggle with self-doubt and could easily lose hope when things don't work out. Find joy in the little things and start counting your blessings in your gratitude journal. Explore your spiritual side by connecting with your intuition through meditation. Focus on the positive and you will find that peace and patience live within you.

Life Path Number 8

8 represents infinity and the power of manifestation. You are a determined person, focused, and thoughtful in all your endeavours. You are confident of your abilities and your realistic, systematic approach is what attracts lucky coincidences to your life.

However, you could be too practical for your good. Learn to drift, dream, and relax your serious demeanour. You could also be too focused on the material aspects of life, thus paying little attention to the spiritual or the emotional. This could lead to a struggle in finding lasting love. You need to sit with your feelings instead of repressing or denying them. Find the root cause of why an emotion feels uncomfortable by writing down what you have learned about each emotion in childhood. Keep removing layer after layer to release the hurt and pain hidden deep inside. Expressing yourself creatively will be very satisfying for you.

Life Path Number 9

9 represents completion and fulfillment. You are likely to gain fame and respect from others through your honourable deeds and inclusive approach. People of all vibrations are attracted to the charisma and magnetism that you effortlessly

emanate. You are someone who can truly attract or manifest all your dreams and goals through positive thinking and harnessing the power of visualization. The shadow side of this aspect could result in emotional blocks, negative thinking, fear, and obsessions. You want to control the outcome of things that could interfere with your soul's plan. Learn to practice present-moment awareness to catch your mind from racing into the unknown and conjuring all sorts of anxious happenings. When in doubt, zoom out and look at the bigger picture.

Life Path Number 11

11 is a powerful master number that represents instinct or faith. You are spiritually gifted, and your soul's purpose is to share the wisdom stored within you with the world. People immediately sense that you are full of inspiring insights. You are likely to have a lot of followers. You know you are here for a reason—to serve and give back to society.

You have a lot to offer, but you could be prone to intense mood swings which could slow your pace. Your inner critic could flare up now and then. Learn to reason with your emotions to find balance in everyday life. Bring out your gratitude journal and appreciate everything that you already have. This will help you manifest the life of your dreams and fulfill your purpose. If you can quieten your mind and its incessant thoughts, you are likely to become a force to reckon with.

Life Path Number 22

22 is a powerful number that represents someone who is an expert builder. You are spiritually gifted, and you have many guides opening up sources of inner power to connect with. Your soul's purpose is to create a better world for our future generation, and that starts with sharing loving-kindness. Your positive approach to life will attract moments of greatness where you can publicly highlight your latent spiritual talents.

The shadow side of this aspect could make you overbearing and self-censoring which could restrict you from using all those hidden spiritual powers. You need to learn to communicate freely and openly with the people in your life to express how you are feeling. Don't hold back from sharing your gifts and talents. This life is the one; communicate your authenticity without fear to tap into your inbuilt power and achieve your ambitions.

Life Path Number 33

33 is the rarest Life Path number that an individual's birthdate can add up to. You are an expert teacher, a powerful healer, and a spiritual leader. You can help bring a positive shift to planet Earth. Your energy draws people in, and you can amass a great deal of positive energy and light vibration to heal, help, or teach others. You are altruistic, empathetic, just, kind, and patient. Always trust your intuition to guide you.

Notice the energy that surges through you when you are working with big groups of people. It is powerful light from the Source you are channelling. This lightwork can drain your physical and emotional bodies. It is important to incorporate periods of rest so your body can recuperate from this powerful lightwork. Put yourself first—heal your wounds and forgive the past so you can serve with a heart full of love.

EXERCISE 7: DECODING YOUR PERSONALITY USING ASTROLOGY

The twelve zodiac constellations according to Western Astrology.

It is believed that Astrology holds the tools that can help heal, transform, and ascend the mind, body, and soul. Human beings have always intuitively felt a connection with the cosmos and the invisible realm of the Universe. The movements of the planets influence our lives just the way solar and lunar cycles affect seasons and the growth of crops. The push and pull of the Moon's energies play with the water bodies on Earth. Considering that human bodies contain up to 60% water, each one of us is unconsciously influenced by these celestial forces.

The sky is divided into twelve zodiac signs, and each sign has a planet, a house, and an element (fire, water, air, or earth) that it rules. The twelve houses represent the basic functions of life. The placement of the sun, the moon, and the planets at the exact moment of your birth creates your natal chart (or birth chart). The place and precise time of your birth are vital in curating an accurate chart.

Your natal chart is an important key to navigating the depths of your character, personality, life cycles, relationship patterns, career, money, and more. It is worth studying as it can reveal quite a lot about yourself that was initially hidden. It acts as a lens to view who you are meant to be, what you are meant to be doing, and how you can get to where your soul wants to go. Your birth chart is like a code or a blueprint that you can use to navigate the course of life. If you pay close attention, it can show details of your future that will manifest in divine timing.

When reading your natal chart, study the characteristics of your sun sign, moon sign, and rising (or ascendant) sign. The sun sign represents the external personality you display to the world, your ego identity, and your role in life. The moon sign represents your emotional self and your hidden world; the side you keep at a distance from others but show to your family and close ones. The rising sign depicts how you come across to people at the first encounter, the mask you wear in public, and those inner motivations that drive you to be who you are.

Your natal chart also reflects how the four Astrological elements influence your life. The four elements symbolize your needs, desires, values, motivations, and orientation toward life. Everyone has their unique balance of these basic energies, better known as their 'elemental makeup'.

Most people's elemental makeup is imbalanced which shows that they are lacking in certain element/s, and this becomes a conscious struggle to overcome. It teaches a lesson to either work harder or appreciate what we already have that we may be ignoring. Sometimes, we overvalue the element we do not have, feeling like we lack something. Other times, we completely neglect it.

Refer to the chart below for the general characteristics each element displays. Which one do you resonate with the most?

Element	Associated Chakra	General Personality
Fire	Solar Plexus chakra	Enthusiastic, active, motivated, inspired, warm
Air	Crown chakra	Intellectual, sociable, curious, studious, witty
Water	Sacral chakra	Intuitive, creative, artistic, empathetic, emotional
Earth	Root chakra	Grounded, secure, practical, realistic, material

Figure 2.1 The four Astrological elements create a comprehensive whole that reflects your unique personality traits.

To calculate your Astrological elemental makeup, explore your birth chart[2] and individually check the elements of each planet.

---

[2] Visit Astrolibrary.org/free-birth-chart/ to study your natal chart in detail. Refer to the list of recommended readings at the end of this book to continue your learning journey into the deep world of Western Astrology.

UNDERSTANDING YOUR ZODIAC SIGN

"What's your zodiac sign?" has to be the most popular icebreaker question out there today. However, it is a myth that each person's sun sign traits exactly define their personality. According to ancient religious manuscripts, the entire zodiac represents a person and each sign needs to be integrated fully for us to become whole.

Each zodiac sign has a respective season that it rules. Aries, Cancer, Libra, and Capricorn are cardinal signs that occur at the start of a new season. Taurus, Leo, Scorpio, and Aquarius are fixed signs that occur in the middle of the season. Gemini, Virgo, Sagittarius, and Pisces are mutable signs that occur at the end of the season.

Cardinal signs are great initiators and leaders. Fixed signs make reliable and steady workers. Mutable signs are fluid and flexible to change.

Ahead, let's explore the general characteristics of each zodiac sign, lucky colour, suggested careers, and more.

Zodiac Sign	Astrological Element	Ruling Months
Aries	Fire	(March 21 – April 19)
Taurus	Earth	(April 20 – May 20)
Gemini	Air	(May 21 – June 20)
Cancer	Water	(June 21 – July 22)
Leo	Fire	(July 23 – August 22)
Virgo	Earth	(August 23 – September 22)
Libra	Air	(September 23 – October 22)
Scorpio	Water	(October 23 – November 21)
Sagittarius	Fire	(November 22 – December 21)
Capricorn	Earth	(December 22 – January 19)

| Aquarius | Air | (January 20 – February 18) |
| Pisces | Water | (February 19 – March 20) |

Figure 2.2 The twelve zodiac signs along with their Astrological elements and ruling months.

Aries (The Ram)

General Characteristics: Aries is the first zodiac sign, and as the designated leader of the pack, they are confident and courageous of the journey ahead. The cardinal fire sign is a natural leader, decisive, and strong-willed. Those born under this sign have an inextinguishable fire burning within that pushes them outside their comfort zone. They are self-starters and initiators who don't wait to take action. An innovator and a risk-taker, Aries is willing to try anything. They are visionaries and pioneers, ready to leave the familiar behind and venture into the unknown. Unafraid and assertive, once Aries makes up their mind, they are most likely to succeed. In relationships, they are charismatic, direct, and dominating. Their dynamic personality and high energy draw people to them, for they truly are one-of-a-kind.

Ruling Planet: Mars
Element: Fire
Quality: Cardinal
Lucky Colour: Red
Gemstone: Diamond
Metal: Iron
Flower: Thistle, Honeysuckle

Suggested Careers: Dentist, Surgeon, Financial Analyst, Principal, Hotel Manager, Construction Worker, Venture Capitalist, Personal Trainer.

Taurus (The Bull)

General Characteristics: Taurus is the second zodiac sign, known for its stability, security, and steadfastness. The fixed earth sign is grounded, determined, and responsible. Those born under this sign have an affinity for luxury and the finer things in life. They love pampering themselves and their close ones, and they like to be surrounded by beauty and nature. Some could even enjoy expressing their creativity through art. They are loyal to their family and friends. When a Taurus commits to a task, they know they will accomplish it. That's how strongly they believe in themselves, and their reliability is what others love about them. In relationships, Taurus is sweet and sensual, expressing their love through meaningful gestures.

Ruling Planet: Venus
Element: Earth
Quality: Fixed
Lucky Colour: Pink
Gemstone: Emerald
Metal: Copper
Flower: Rose

Suggested Careers: Fashion Designer, Interior Designer, Landscaping, Banker, Financial Advisor, Manager, Restaurateur, Sommelier, Furniture Maker.

Gemini (The Twins)

General Characteristics: Gemini is the third zodiac sign, known for its strong communication skills and twin personality. The mutable air sign is quick-witted, intelligent, and friendly. Gemini is insatiably curious and intellectually driven; they love reading and learning new things that provide mental stimulation, and no topic is off the table for them. They thrive in social situations as they love meeting new people, exchanging stories, and expressing ideas. This sign represents duality and diversity. There are always two sides to a Gemini, and their opposite personalities can either clash or complement each other. In relationships, they are rational, adaptable, and flexible to their partner's needs.

Ruling Planet: Mercury
Element: Air
Quality: Mutable
Lucky Colour: Yellow

Gemstone: Agate
Metal: Mercury
Flower: Lily of the Valley

Suggested Careers: Teacher, Interpreter, Public Relations, Translator, Journalist, Project Manager, Communications Specialist, Makeup Artist, Stylist.

Cancer (The Crab)

General Characteristics: Cancer, the fourth zodiac sign, is known for motherhood, home, and family life. The cardinal water sign is nurturing, empathetic, oversensitive, and intuitive. They will go all out to make their home as serene and comfortable as possible. They are fiercely protective of their family and friends as they are devoted to them. Those born under this sign are sincere, warm, and gentle in their demeanour, though they can get possessive and controlling with their close ones. Cancerians care deeply, and their soft heart can get hurt easily. They tend to remember old hurts and can hold grudges. It's best to forgive and forget the past, and when a Cancerian finally decides to do that, they jump back to being their loyal, playful self.

Ruling Planet: Moon
Element: Water
Quality: Cardinal
Lucky Colour: Silver
Gemstone: Pearl
Metal: Silver
Flower: Acanthus

Suggested Careers: Nurse, Doctor, Caterer, Content Manager, Teacher, Speech Therapist, Social Worker, Antique Dealer, Author.

Leo (The Lion)

General Characteristics: Leo is the fifth zodiac sign. Just like a lion, Leos are self-confident, bold, and extroverted. The fixed fire sign is energetic, passionate, and motivated. Those born under this sign have a magnetic personality and they seem to become the centre of attention in every room. They are confident communicators and are unlikely to shy away from public speaking opportunities. They will never say no to an adventure. Leos are flamboyant, dramatic, and sometimes ostentatious because they want to stand out from the crowd. They are born leaders, and they shine bright in their workplaces. In relationships, Leos love to luxuriously pamper their partner. They are noble, generous, and big-hearted, and always leave a lasting impression.

Ruling Planet: Sun
Element: Fire
Quality: Fixed
Lucky Colour: Yellow
Gemstone: Ruby
Metal: Gold
Flower: Sunflower

Suggested Careers: Actor, Designer, Event Planner, Marketer, Sales Representative, Teacher, Inspirational Speaker, Public Relations.

Virgo (The Virgin)
General Characteristics: Virgo is the sixth zodiac sign, known for its exact and detailed approach to life. The mutable earth sign is practical, grounded, and cautious. Those born under this sign are methodical and efficient at work and at home. Their critical nature is driven by perfectionism, for they like to excel in everything they do. Virgos are born to serve and give back however they can. In relationships, they are kind, modest, and trustworthy. This sign is associated with organization and improvement. Virgos are hard-working, disciplined, and organized. They will patiently work through obstacles and know that every problem always has a solution. They just need more time to find it.

Ruling Planet: Mercury
Element: Earth
Quality: Mutable
Lucky Colour: Green
Gemstone: Sardonyx
Metal: Nickel
Flower: Anemone

Suggested Careers: Researcher, Investor, Therapist, Statistician, Machinist, Manager, Chemist, Perfume Maker, Cocktail Mixologist, Landscaper.

Libra (The Scales)

General Characteristics: Libra is the seventh zodiac sign, known for its balanced approach to life. This cardinal air sign is just and fair in everything they do and with everyone they meet. Librans are exact and precise, in their thoughts, words, and actions. Their mind is always measuring, weighing the pros and cons of every decision they make. When faced with a multitude of options to choose from, Libra can be rather indecisive. Those born under this sign are diplomatic, ethical, and equal. They are drawn to intellectual pursuits and the arts, and some could be quite artistic themselves. Librans are well-equipped with strong communication skills and are innovative in their work projects. Relationships and partnerships weigh the most in a Libran's life because once they make a decision, it's final.

Ruling Planet: Venus
Element: Air
Quality: Cardinal
Lucky Colour: Blue
Gemstone: Sapphire
Metal: Copper
Flower: Rose

Suggested Careers: Human Resources Manager, Legal Analyst, Buyer, Event Planner, Business Owner, Museum Curator, Cultural Critic, Graphic Designer, Pro-Bono Lawyer.

Scorpio (The Scorpion)

General Characteristics: Scorpio is the eighth zodiac sign, known for its love of mystery, passion, and secrets. This fixed water sign is unafraid of the unknown and is intrigued by the ideas of death and rebirth. They understand that metamorphosis requires changing shape or form, and are willing to upgrade their internal values or external appearances to better reflect their mood or state of mind. Scorpio is an interpersonal sign that values intimate relationships and emotional bonds. Sex is a riveting subject for a Scorpio; they could either be dominating or submissive to their partner. They are loyal lovers, but if spurned, have the ability to wreak havoc through revenge. Though moments of despair and dark thoughts can cloud up a Scorpio's mind, forgiveness holds the key to freeing the heaviness in their hearts.

Ruling Planet: Pluto
Element: Water
Quality: Fixed
Lucky Colour: Dark Red
Gemstone: Opal
Metal: Steel or Iron
Flower: Geranium

Suggested Careers: Psychologist, Physician, Engineer, Market Analyst, Financial Advisor, Surgeon, Psychologist, Social Worker, Detective, Archaeologist.

Sagittarius (The Archer)

General Characteristics: Sagittarius is the ninth zodiac sign. The archer shoots an arrow high up in the sky, following its trajectory as it ascends into higher dimensions. Known for its love for travel and philosophy, this mutable fire sign is born with wanderlust and a desire to explore different cultures. Represented by a centaur who is half human and half horse, this restless adventurer longs to roam wild and free. Optimistic and outgoing, Sagittarians are quick to make friends and enthusiastically preach their 'one life, live it large' philosophy. Their independent streak shows up in relationships, reminding them to make time for introspection. Those born under this sign are religiously or spiritually inclined, choosing to follow their internal quest until they find all the answers to life's mysteries.

Ruling Planet: Jupiter
Element: Fire
Quality: Mutable
Lucky Colour: Purple
Gemstone: Topaz
Metal: Tin
Flower: Carnation

Suggested Careers: Brand Ambassador, Public Relations Manager, Development Officer, Instructor, Investigator, Travel Agent, Personal Trainer, Travel Guide, Pilot, Teacher, Preacher.

Capricorn (The Goat)

General Characteristics: Capricorn is the tenth zodiac sign, known for its hardworking nature and steadfastness. This fixed air sign is punctilious and calculative in making decisions, constantly seeking excellence in everything they attempt. The goat is slow and cautious while climbing the mountain, but knows that perseverance and resilience guide the way to the top. Thanks to their innate ability to manage responsibility, Capricorns make high achievers and great leaders who impart wisdom through their teachings. In relationships, they are realistic, grounded, patient, and prudent. However, their serious demeanour and businesslike approach can make them appear cold and aloof. Those born under this sign are ambitious and driven to perform; their confident and disciplined mindset ensures they emerge victorious and achieve their goals.

Ruling Planet: Saturn
Element: Earth
Quality: Cardinal
Lucky Colour: Dark Grey, Black
Gemstone: Amethyst
Metal: Lead
Flower: Ivy

Suggested Careers: Manager, Consultant, Accountant, Banker, Financial Planner, Nurse, Teacher, Computer Programmer, Professional Organizer.

Aquarius (The Water Bearer)

General Characteristics: Aquarius is the eleventh zodiac sign, known as the futuristic visionary or the new-age thinker. This fixed air sign has a keen desire to make this world a better place. They are one step ahead of the rest, and often have ground-breaking ideas and innovative thoughts that may seem too progressive. Those born under this sign are the movers and shakers; they push old, limiting structures by envisioning new, boundless realities. Their interest in humanitarianism gives them a philanthropic side, and their sharp wit and intellect make them strong communicators. In relationships, though Aquarians are staunchly independent and emotionally detached from their environment, their loyalty doesn't sway. Their unconventional approach to life could see them refusing to pay heed to societal norms, choosing to stay unpredictable in their farsighted thinking.

Ruling Planet: Uranus (Formerly Saturn)
Element: Air
Quality: Fixed
Lucky Colour: Turquoise
Gemstone: Aquamarine
Metal: Aluminum
Flower: Orchid

Suggested Careers: Trainer, Environmental Engineer, Mediator, Actor, Scientist, Data Analyst, Astronaut, Inventor, Technological Innovator, Skydiving Instructor, Radical Activist.

Pisces (The Fish)

General Characteristics: Pisces is the twelfth and the last zodiac sign that brings us to the end of the astrological cycle. This mutable water sign holds the wisdom and characteristics of all the other eleven zodiac signs. Those born under this sign are deeply emotional and spiritual, swimming between different realms of illusion and reality. They prefer to live in their world of imagination, for their creative minds cannot function in the monotony of everyday life. In relationships, this dreamy vibe may come across as the fish being elusive and escapist, but it is simply seeking the quiet safety of muddy waters. Just like water, Pisces seems to flow from place to place, trusting the process and flexibly adapting to change. Pisceans are naturally intuitive and are drawn to the occult and esoteric sciences. They are compassionate and altruistic, selflessly giving to those in need.

Ruling Planet: Neptune (Formerly Jupiter)
Element: Water
Quality: Mutable
Lucky Colour: Sea Green
Gemstone: Moonstone
Metal: Platinum
Flower: Water Lily

Suggested Careers: Writer, Poet, Recruiter, Physical Therapist, Social Worker, Salesperson, Healer, Spiritual Leader, Musician, Photographer.

Chapter 4

...❖...

NAVIGATING YOUR CHOSEN CAREER PATH

Destiny. Fate. Maktub. Kismet.

Your career may seem like a choice you made. Perhaps your parents decided on a career path for you. It could be utterly serendipitous or a well-planned trajectory that brought you to where you are today. Maybe you are not working or are a student not sure of what career to pursue.

Needless of where you are in your life path, the truth is that each one of us has a purpose or a calling to fulfill. It is written in your soul's contract by your Higher Self before you incarnate on Earth.

There are special gifts your soul has that are needed on Earth right now. These gifts are unique to you; there is no one quite like yourself who can offer those exact skills. These talents are carried forward from your past lives and sometimes, a soul can spend multiple lifetimes honing one skill before becoming an expert at it.

How do you know what your soul's talents are? Those qualities simply shine. Everyone praises you for it because it comes so naturally to you. These gifts are usually showcased when you are young.

However, you have to overcome karmic challenges before you can start sharing your unique gifts with the world. These karmic challenges are set out by your Higher Self in your soul's contract for your present life.

Souls who can utilize their unique gifts and talents in their careers are the most successful. They have infused purpose with their passion—their lives shine with meaning.

Take, for example, Steve Jobs, who was one of the greatest innovators and visionaries of our time. When Jobs was fired from his own company, he did not lose faith. He started another company NeXt, later bought by Apple, which returned Jobs to the spotlight. Despite facing rejection, Jobs followed his passion. The secret is to do what you love and love what you do.

Some souls have become lost or complacent in their careers. They settle into a comfortable place where they give up working toward their soul's goals. Many are working in a 9-5 job that is not serving their higher purpose. That is why they feel energetically drained, listless, and depressed.

For others, money has become the driving motivation. Such souls have lost touch with their true gifts and passions, and instead, they are following a meaningless path that eventually leads them to feel stuck, sick, and stressed.

Money is not the end goal. Your end goal is to gain enlightenment and attain *moksha.*

Money is just a form of currency that is only valid on Earth. Money is a social construct just like time; we should tend to both very carefully. Hoarding money blocks its flow because money is energy.

You are not going to carry your money into the spiritual realm. You are going to leave your money for your family on Earth.

Money and time do not exist in the spiritual realm. What exists is light consciousness that radiates love, peace, and harmony.

Money is an energetic form created by human beings to exert their power and authority on others. This has resulted in a huge divide between the rich and the poor. The middle class is always striving to be richer, but it is the wrong goal. If we make money our goal, we are not going to end up feeling happy. It is like a dog chasing its tail or a rat caught in a trap. This is my soul's experience not just in this lifetime, but in past lifetimes as well. Money is not going to bring you happiness. If you want abundance in your life, change your thinking patterns and follow your passion. Money will flow into your life.

If you remember your true potential—the fact that you are a co-creator of your life's journey—you will live each moment with light-hearted abandon and joy, knowing there is no future that you are working towards. With this approach, every moment becomes an opportunity to tap into love, joy, inner peace, and gratitude.

If you have not found your passion in life yet, keep looking for it. Don't settle for mundane work. Don't ever give up on your dreams. Growth will not happen unless we step outside our comfort zone. Infuse your life with creativity and make your life a work of art. You are neither too old nor too young to pursue your hobbies. If you work hard for it, success will find you.

In this lifetime, I was blessed with gifts that appeared prominently in my childhood. In school, I was introverted and I spent most of my time reading books. I enjoyed studying literature and writing poetry. I loved the English language, and this slowly paved the way for me to emerge as a journalist. Once school ended, I had a plethora of options to choose from for higher studies. At one point, I wanted to pursue a career in biotechnology. Next, I was convinced law was the right career for me. Hotel management seemed to be my calling as well. A bachelor's degree in business administration was an equally tantalizing subject to study. I was drawn to many pathways I wanted to explore. In hindsight, none of them were meant for me.

As I was graduating from high school, my English teacher advised my parents to let me pursue my love for writing. This brought my parents to decide on journalism. Somehow, my parents were guided by my high school teacher as well as their Higher Selves who knew what my career path was going to be. Would my life have been the same if I pursued law or hotel management? Most definitely not, as I would have spent my life doing something I wasn't interested in.

Soon enough, I landed my first internship with *Hindustan Times,* a leading daily newspaper in India. The editor admired my sense of style and recognized my interest in fashion, and she encouraged me to cover and report on that beat. That's how I decided to pursue my master's degree in fashion journalism.

Another synchronicity worth recounting from *Hindustan Times:* I interned under a fashion columnist who years later hired me to work on her team at *Elle India*, and a few years after that recommended me at *Vogue India* where I worked as the senior fashion writer.

With perspective, I can see it was all divinely connected, every part of it. Everyone I met on my journey was part of my soul's contract—they were all my karmic soul teachers.

Although I was in charge of my career, I felt as if a higher power was pulling the strings, orchestrating the whole scenario. This higher power gently nudged me on the journey ahead, and I realized I just had to trust my intuition and follow the path from one karmic soul teacher to another.

Another meaningful coincidence transpired on my 21st birthday when my friends in college gifted me a Tarot deck. I had always been fascinated by the occult and esoteric sciences but I never thought I would learn how to read Tarot cards. When I got the deck, I knew it was meant to be. I started practicing Tarot readings for myself and my close friends for the next few years. Everyone I read cards for told me they resonated with Tarot's messages. The cards accurately described what was happening in their lives and guided the future. For those not acquainted with the art of Tarot, the 78 cards contain secret teachings of mystery schools in ancient Egypt. The illustrations for the 22 Major Arcana cards are synonymous with a course in personal and spiritual development. The images on the Tarot cards connect to ancient religious beliefs and mythologies, especially the Hebrew Kabbalah. The numbers on the cards tie into the teachings of Pythagoras, who as we explored in chapter 2, believed numbers contained sacred wisdom.

When I moved from Mumbai to Toronto, I started life afresh. Quitting my dream job was very hard for me, and now I faced the decision to choose between fashion and spirituality as a career. After spending years working in the fashion industry, I realized my spiritual gifts were not utilized. My soul longed to delve deeper into spiritual studies, meditation and practicing healing modalities. It was hard to leave my dream life that I had been relishing for so long, but I knew I had to shed my skin to begin a brand-new journey.

That's when I decided to launch Svetarot - Tarot, Oracle and Crystal Healing Services (svetarotreading.com). I enrolled myself in a Tarot certification course and after becoming a certified Tarot reader, I started conducting 1:1 sessions on Zoom that would allow me to hold space and guide people through any questions they have related to their life, relationships, marriage, career, health, or finances. After I was booked by 100+ people for Tarot sessions, I felt encouraged to follow my spiritual calling.

Tarot and Oracle cards are one healing modality I use to understand the client's psyche and help them connect with their Higher Self. The main purpose of Tarot is to see what the future has in store, but it is important to remember that the future is not set in stone. The future is created by the actions you are taking in this present moment, and if you change your present actions, you can change your future. So, at the time of the reading, the cards reflect a future that is based on the present actions that you are taking. Tarot has served as a tool to connect with my Higher Self that guides me onto the right path. It has helped me understand patterns in my life and my relationships with people, and it has stimulated my intuitive powers and deepened my understanding of life. Someone once asked me if Tarot was black magic. This level of ignorance made me understand that people are scared of the unknown—which includes secret knowledge only in the hands of a few—and some can be spooked when the Tarot sheds light on their life with profound accuracy.

Crystals are another modality I incorporate—I advise clients on the crystals to wear based on a chakra reading. I also design customized bracelets or necklaces to activate and balance chakras. The idea of venturing into jewellery design was a childhood dream that saw the light of day through my Etsy store, Svetarot Jewellery.

I was able to create my dream career around my passion for writing, designing jewellery, reading Tarot, and helping people, and so can you. I believe in chasing your dreams and living a life fueled by passion, and I recommend you follow what your inner voice is saying to you. The question is: are you listening?

This is why your chosen career path is so important. If you are spending your 9-5 doing something you are not interested in, you are going to feel depressed, anxious, and confused. You are not going to attract the right colleagues at your workplace. The Universe will give you hints that you are not happy, but you will not want to quit. When you are not happy, you are not going to be making a lot of money. Your self-worth will fall lower, and you will end this life feeling unfulfilled. The crux of the matter is to start doing things that genuinely bring you joy. Align your day job with your passion to open the gates of happiness.

If you are not feeling joyous in your day job, quit it. You deserve it. You need to be doing things that are important to you. You only have limited time here, and if your job is bringing you monotony, it is not going to bring you inner peace.

Sometimes we get so caught up in the travails of life that we forget to take notice of the small things that are happening right before us. Those small things are the ones that add up in retrospect. After all, you can only connect the dots looking backward. So, trust in the process and stay in the present moment. Be aware and focus on what is happening in the now and believe that things will work out.

11 WAYS TO BE HAPPIER AT WORK

Lighten up your day with these tips that are sure to get your day moving forward positively.

1. Start your day with positive affirmations
How you feel in the morning has a direct impact on how productive you are throughout the day. If you set positive intentions for the day ahead right in the morning, you are likely to stay in that optimistic frame of mind throughout your day ensuring positive work relations, better performance at work, and inner satisfaction.
Tip: Saying "Thank you" as soon as your feet hit the ground first thing in the morning will kick-start your day with gratitude.

2. Help out a co-worker
Helping other people feels good and it increases your happiness quotient while lowering your stress levels. Plus, volunteering to help someone starts a cycle of good karma which enhances your self-esteem, boosts your mental health, and gives you a positive perspective on life.
Tip: Offer help to colleagues, volunteer in your free time, or perform random acts of kindness.

3. Monitor your progress every week
One of the most motivational activities to boost morale at work is noting the progress you are making every week. Yes, we all have big projects and even bigger dreams to achieve, but acknowledging the small steps taken daily and then reflecting on your progress after the week is over will imbibe a can-do spirit in you. This will lift you on days you are feeling low.
Tip: Maintaining a diary with weekly achievements will help record all your successes in one place.

4. Have an end goal

Knowing where you are right now and where you want to go is all you need to be clear about. The end goal is the dream you wish to achieve or the long-term plan you have. Simply having the final result in your mind will put you on the right track and help you focus on what is truly important.
Tip: Visualize your end goal in your mind daily, and believe you are there already. You soon will be.

5. Eat healthily and stay hydrated

Eating a light lunch will ensure you are not fatigued when it is 4 pm while skipping carbohydrates will make sure your energy levels don't crash resulting in you feeling irritated and tired. Try maintaining a healthy diet with balanced proportions. Sipping on water throughout the day will keep your mind active and improve concentration.
Tip: Track your water and food intake using a fitness app.

6. Swap multitasking for mindfulness

Focusing on multiple things at once will lead to you completing none. Make a to-do list and focus your energies on one item at a time, and while doing it, give it your 100% attention. Not only will this bring about optimal efficiency, but boost your productivity levels as well.
Tip: Prioritize your tasks.

7. Learn to let go of control

Clients will always want changes, companies may back out from that important merger, and your colleague may mess up an important task—it is Murphy's law. Accepting that we cannot control external circumstances will give you an inner peace you did not know existed within you. We are beings of duality; what goes on the inside reflects on the outside.
Tip: Once you let go of what the outcome should be, you start controlling the situation through detachment.

8. Set aside some time for personal tasks
Everyone has personal responsibilities, and if there is a pressing matter to deal with, it is better to wrap that up first than let it affect your work. For that reason, putting aside as little as 20-30 minutes in your day for personal tasks will give you much-needed peace of mind.
Tip: Fix a suitable time that you will dedicate to yourself and stick to it every day.

9. Take time to relax periodically
It is very easy to get distracted when you are working, which is why inculcating a habit of taking a five-minute break every hour will help you re-focus. You could walk around the office or at home if you work remotely, chat with a colleague, listen to your favourite song, or even meditate. This will boost your concentration powers and give you a sense of freedom when you take regular breaks.
Tip: Practice deep breathing. The oxygen flowing through your mind and body will awaken your senses.

10. Stay true to yourself
Know that shortcuts are not the way to success—hard work and perseverance will take you there. Remember the reason you are working, what fulfills your passion, and what gets you going. Your career is going to be long and tiring, but if you remember to stay true to yourself, your hard work will pay off.
Tip: Honesty is the best policy.

11. End your workday with gratitude
Just the way you begin your day with positive affirmations, end your day with gratitude. Give heartfelt thanks to all your colleagues, for the work you were able to finish, and lastly, to yourself.
Tip: Smile and laugh as much as you can every day.

Part 2

Chapter 5

. . ❖ . .

DELVING INTO PAST LIVES AND REMEMBERING SOUL MATES

Have you ever met someone for the first time and felt an instant connection? They are most likely your soul mate from a past life.

Exploring past lives[3] is important because you need to know where your soul originates from. When you delve into your past lives, you will notice the recent ones will come back to you very quickly. The ancient ones will be buried deep within your soul's memories, and they will not come to your awareness easily. The past lives that come up are the ones that are highly impacting your life right now. Keep digging deeper until you discover your soul's wisdom on your karmic relationship patterns.

Your life story is your journey that is as unique as your soul's blueprint. From your name to your date of birth, your soul chooses each element before you were born on Earth.

Choosing to incarnate on Earth is a difficult choice. Earth is a difficult school, and one glance at today's headlines in the news will confirm that.

---

[3] If you would like to learn more about your soul and your real identity, try a past-life regression led by a trained past-life therapist.

Countries are at war, gun violence is on the rise, the chasm between poor and rich people is ever-increasing, climate change is causing unrepairable damage to our planet, and gender inequality and racial discrimination are rampant... the list goes on.

Over all these years, and lifetimes, wars, and the way that humanity has evolved, it has created distrust among our own family of humans. We turned against each other and we stopped participating in actions that brought us joy. We forgot that we are creative souls, call it the amnesia we have. So, why would we die and come back?

We return to Earth because we have unfulfilled karmic contracts with our soul mates and soul family members. Before incarnating, we choose our parents, siblings, friends, and life partner. These are all members of your soul family you share karma with. Each soul moves in circles with its soul group or family members with whom it has karmic contracts to fulfill.

Karma is not punishment; it is the law of cause and effect. Positive actions bring good karma, and negative actions bring bad karma. Since we usually live in auto-pilot mode, we are unaware of our actions and the impact it has on others. Being kind to everyone, giving back, and living in harmony can help improve your soul's karma.

Every person in your life—be it your parents, siblings, best friend, favourite aunt, or even a school teacher—is divinely connected to your soul's purpose. They are all ultimately part of a larger soul group, though individually each soul may have different karmic contracts to fulfill with each other. As we go through each life on Earth, we unintentionally and unconsciously get caught up in karmic debt with some souls.

*A soul chooses its mother first, and the mother picks
the father. A karmic contract is signed between the
three souls to carry out their roles responsibly.*

When a soul comes back with a new ego identity in the next life, it writes out its life's story in a way that will involve these soul mates so that each can repay karmic debt. These are soul contracts made in the spirit world between your soul and your soul mates. Karmic debt is exchanged through roles that these soul mates play out. Some could play a positive role, while others are bound by contract to teach you and challenge you to evolve.

The actions of your last birth connect to your present life. If your soul hurt or harmed another soul in the past, then you will be paying off your debt to them in this birth. Some souls wait for lifetimes spanning thousands of years to recreate scenarios on Earth where both souls can come together to repay their karmic debt.

Now that we recognize that everyone in our life is there for a reason, let's not discount their presence. Learn to work in tandem with their vibrational energies, no matter whether it is low or high. If you are not in a good mood one day and you lash out at your family member, the next day, their bruised ego could throw the same bad vibe back at you. So, learn to break this pattern and be cognizant that these soul mates are there in our lives to teach us and help us grow. The main reason we meet each other in this Earthly school is to rub off on each other and show each other the path to enlightenment so we can break out of this karmic cycle of reincarnation.

It is very important to understand that every relationship in our life is like a mirror. They are showing us what we are showing them. This is the hard truth that is so difficult to digest and implement in our lives. If we are showing them gratitude, love, and light, they will reflect it to us.

If it is an unenlightened relationship where only one partner is self-aware or spiritually awakened, then the other could keep bringing negativity and unhealed wounds into the relationship. However, if your soul is emanating a high vibration of love and peace, you are not going to be affected by another person's low vibration. After all, if we are all connected and part of one big soul family, why would you waste your precious time and energy hating or fighting people? You are not going to be carrying resentment forward into your life, remembering past wounds they inflicted upon you. You would see their suffering and practice heartfelt forgiveness to break the karmic bonds between you two by bringing in unconditional love to melt all anger, hurt, and pain.

It is vital to be aware of these repetitive patterns that we have with our parents, siblings, and our friends. Not only is this an indicator of the relationship that you share with yourself but it is also shedding light on the relationship karma that you have with your soul mates in this life.

Most people wear a mask in public. They show friends and acquaintances their best personalities, but their nature is different with their partner, parents, or siblings. It is interesting to note that the biggest karmic contracts each soul has are with its immediate family members. No wonder some siblings cannot stand each other—their souls could be enemies from a past life that have now reincarnated to bring harmony between them.

When did we adopt this idea of wearing our ego identity 24/7 and never dropping the mask? It is time to remember the real reason we are here—to evolve into a compassionate and loving soul emanating peace and harmony. It is time to avoid fueling drama and do the inner healing work.

If you can work through your karma and transmute it, your next life will be easier and free of conflict in the challenging areas that you face in your current life.

Sometimes, souls get way ahead of themselves while preparing their soul contracts before incarnating, and plan a grandiose scheme wherein they hope to master all the lessons they need to. These souls almost always set themselves up for failure, for it can take a soul multiple lifetimes to absorb the teachings of one lesson. Take, for example, the lesson of honesty. Are you truly transparent with the people in your life? More importantly, are you honest with yourself? It is difficult for many. Any soul who has sinned knows that. Thieves, con artists, and those deceiving souls who prey on innocent lives live in a world of sheer ignorance, where they are isolated from their Higher Selves. They believe no one is watching them as they commit felonies, lie, cheat, and betray others. Sadly, their Higher Self is noting every action with disappointment, fully aware that the soul will have to pay for the negative karma it is accumulating.

Just because the soul was not strong enough to surpass the temptation of wrongdoing, the noble plan of leading an honest life it had penned before its incarnation on Earth goes awry, and the soul falls into a pit of darkness. Dark nights of the soul occur. In such circumstances, a soul's Higher Self often sets up rude awakenings in the form of accidents and misfortunate events. This is a sign that a soul has fallen off the path it had originally set out to walk on.

Help is always available, and the Universe is unconditionally forgiving. Repent for any sins or mistakes your soul has committed intentionally or unintentionally. Seek forgiveness for your actions. Be honest with yourself and sincere in your spiritual journey.

Ahead, let's go deeper into understanding your relationship patterns.

EXERCISE 8: DECODING YOUR SOUL'S RELATIONSHIP KARMA

Before you begin writing, ground yourself by visualizing a bright white light surrounding your body. This powerful healing light cleanses and refreshes you completely.

Now, write down the first thoughts that come to you.

Growing up, what was your relationship like with your parents?

_____

_____

_____

_____

_____

_____

What are your relationships like with the people in your life?

_____

_____

_____

_____

_____

_____

When was the last time you experienced conflict in a close relationship? How did you handle it?

_____

_____

_____

_____

_____

_____

Are you dependent on others or independent of others?

_____

_____

_____

_____

_____

_____

What are some recurring issues you face in your relationships?

_____

_____

_____

_____

_____

What actions can you take to improve the state of your relationships?

_____

_____

_____

_____

_____

_____

Great job on completing this exercise. You are doing so well! Bringing awareness to your immediate relationships can help you understand how you come across to people, and how your actions are impacting them. Remember, we are mirrors of each other. If you don't like something about someone else, it is most likely an aspect you don't like about yourself. Forgive yourself and forgive others. Love yourself and love others. That is the only way we can bring harmony to planet Earth.

Now, let's delve deeper into soul mate recognition and the types of soul mates you will meet on your journey.

HOW TO RECOGNIZE SOUL MATES

All it takes is one glance for soul recognition to happen. The eyes are the window to the soul and when you look deeply into their eyes, your soul will remember theirs. You feel a sense of familiarity like you know them from before.

Are there people in your life you feel you were destined to meet or those who make you feel at home when you're around them? These are people with whom you share a strong soul connection. They are part of your soul family. The same souls might occasionally trigger you and contribute to your most transformational wounds. Every experience is meant to awaken you through pain and suffering, with the goal of mastering lessons that advance your soul's growth.

Meeting soul mates can be triggering—it can bring up both happiness and suffering, depending on the positive or negative karma you share with them. If the karma shared is positive, the relationship will feel supportive and easy to handle. You will want to spend more time together because of how good it feels to be in each other's company. What is happening here is that your chakras are aligning with theirs, creating a magnetic frequency that attracts you to each other and binds you together.
If the karma shared is negative, the relationship will experience moments of conflict when both souls will be tested on their lessons. Anger, resentment, and other negative feelings can arise. This karma needs to be transmuted by both parties and the quickest path to doing that is by forgiving the other person. Forgiveness sets both souls free.

You may not share karma with everyone in your life, but you can create new karmic bonds with souls you enter into a romantic relationship with.

Every relationship must be treated with care and respect for it holds the key to peace and enlightenment.

Each soul has 6 soul mates that together make up a soul family of 7. 7 soul families together make up a soul group of 49 souls. Soul groups tend to incarnate together as the progress of each group depends on the overall progress of each soul. In other words, a soul group will not be able to reach ascension if one of its soul members is stuck in the lower realms. Therefore, it is essential to empower your soul mates as you will not be able to evolve to the next stage without them.

People that enter your life coincidentally choose to intervene for a higher divine purpose. I remember reuniting with a dear childhood friend after many years. As soon as our eyes met, I felt like we had known each other before. Of course, we had known each other as children, but this was different. I was certain that our souls knew each other from a past life. This connection tugged at my heart, and I was intrigued to try a past life session with a regression therapist. The session confirmed that we had indeed incarnated centuries ago in an ancient lifetime in France. The positive karmic bond from that lifetime got carried forward to this present lifetime. Another powerful moment of soul recognition occurred when I met a friend's childhood friend. Though we had nothing in common and neutral karma to share, I recognized their soul by looking into their eyes. Upon confiding this intuitive knowledge with them, they confirmed that they too sensed the immense familiarity.

Do we just have one soul mate? No. We have multiple soul mates. In fact, everyone in your life right now is your soul mate. It does not have to be a romantic connection—it can be a family member, a relative, a childhood friend, a colleague, a business partner, etc. Soul mates enter your life in a synchronistic manner, and their presence serves a purpose.

Most of the time when souls come back together, they are looking to heal from past hurts you caused them or they caused you and do a better job at playing their chosen role with your soul. It is up to you to discern whether their presence is taking away your peace or adding to it. Remember, any conflict or discord in karmic relationships can be dissolved through practicing non-judgmental love and unconditional forgiveness.

Let's look at the different types of soul mate connections that you can experience in an Earthly lifetime.

1. Twin Flames or Twin Souls

This is the other half of your soul. When a soul begins its journey, it is split into a male and female form. Both souls strive to reunite after paying their karmic debt to form the whole soul and attain enlightenment in this Universe. Twin flame relationships can challenge, teach, heal, and love in powerful ways. Meeting your twin serves as a catalyst that brings about a massive change in your life and shifts your vibration into a higher one. When twin souls find each other, synchronicities abound.

2. Divine Mother and Divine Father Souls

This set of souls is part of your team of guardians on planet Earth. When your soul incarnates in a human body, it is very vulnerable to external influences. The divine mother and divine father accept the responsibility of nourishing and caring for your body until your soul is ready to take over and step into its higher purpose. The divine mother shares a telepathic connection with her child and any intuitive soul can tap into this.

3. Karmic Soul Partners

This is the life partner (or partners) your soul chose before you incarnated on Earth. It is usually a significant romantic connection. It could signify a positive, uplifting relationship where both souls bloom together or a toxic relationship where both souls feed off each other. The lesson is always to help each other heal past wounds and evolve through unconditional love. Karmic soul partners challenge us in intimate ways to shed our ego identity and step into our soul identity.

4. Karmic Soul Teachers

These are teachers, healers, mentors, practitioners, spiritual guides, and influential leaders who enter your life to teach you divine lessons. It could be your high school teacher you fondly reminisce about or a famous spiritual guru whose teachings you follow on social media. This archetype appears in every soul's life and creates profound learning experiences that help foster growth. It's important to remember that ultimately, we are all students in this Earthly realm, and as souls, it is our inherent nature to grow and evolve.

5. Karmic Soul Mates

These are your fellow soul mates attending the same Earthly school as you. The relationship you share could be positive, negative, or neutral. Each soul mate is on its unique path, and you both may share good, bad, or neutral karma. It is up to your Higher Self to determine the state of the relationship, and instruct you whether to follow through with it or not. When dealing with your karmic soul mate relationships, always tune in to your heart to connect with your intuition to understand whether their intentions are good or bad.

6. Soul Crossings

These are special experiences or spiritual awakenings you share with someone for a short period before destiny steps in to cause separation. Everything about this relationship feels like a meaningful coincidence as if you were meant to meet for a reason. However, the timing, the place, or the situation does not allow a long-term relationship, and soon you both go on separate paths. The lesson here is that love is universal and not timebound, but we cannot hold on to people as they have their journeys to focus on.

7. Kindred Spirits

These are like-minded souls who understand you and share the same values as you. You feel peaceful in their presence, and you have a lot in common. You learn more about yourself through them and you could intuitively know what they are thinking or feeling. These soul-ships are not bound by karma, time, age, or gender. It could be a fleeting smile shared with a stranger, a short conversation with someone that inspires you to change, or a kind person who helped you out in a time of need.

CASE STUDY 1 – A STORY OF TWIN SOULS: SAM AND SARA

Let's explore some life incidents to better understand how soul contracts work and the role soul family members play in a soul's life.

Sam is an only child, and his parents dote on him. He shares a deep connection with his mother and the two of them share a telepathic bond. Growing up, Sam always adheres to their wishes and follows the path they set out for him. When he decides to pursue law, he moves away from his childhood home to be on his own for the first time.

At college, Sam is introduced to Sara. The moment he locks eyes with her, there is an instant sense of familiarity that makes him feel that he knows her from before. Sara is a shy girl, whose parents passed away when she was young. Her aunt brought her up in a protective environment where she was not allowed to make her own choices. Being at college, away from her controlling aunt, Sara is free to choose and navigate her life according to her wishes. When she meets Sam, she feels a strange pull toward him. Around him, she can relax and be her true self without any judgment. Sam feels a tremendous need to protect Sara, and within no time, the two are inseparable.

Upon graduating, Sam is offered a job in a different city. He is elated to begin his career, but his parents want him to move back and live with them. Sam feels his parents are being unreasonable. His conversations with his parents are now strained, and he feels disconnected from them.

His parents feel lonely without him, and his mother's health is deteriorating. Sam decides to visit his parents. He brings Sara along to introduce her to them. On his way back to his hometown, he reflects on how his life has changed ever since he first left home. He is now in a committed relationship and happy with his chosen career. He feels proud of how far he has come, but he recognizes a gnawing pain within. He knows he has neglected his parents, especially his mother, and he is aware that he needs to heal his relationship with them.

When Sam reaches home, he is aghast—his mother is sick and in a frail condition. Sam's father reveals his mother is suffering from a life-threatening disease. Sam is overcome with guilt, and he blames himself for his negligent behaviour.

His mother is elated upon seeing Sam, but she instantly forms a strong dislike for Sara. They bicker about his relationship but cannot reach a compromise.

Days pass; Sam and Sara's relationship starts to take a toll. A guilt-ridden Sam inadvertently takes out his anger on Sara for coming in between him and his parents.

Sara, who always looked up to him, lashes out with a victim mentality and decides to leave. She returns to her aunt's home, joins a new job, and promises herself that she will never contact Sam.

A heartbroken Sam extends his stay at home and eventually decides to quit his job to take care of his mother. The next few months are tough—his heart longs to be with Sara, but he also knows his mother needs him. This ongoing battle to choose between the two eats away at him, and he slowly starts losing interest in everyday living.

Sam's father, who has always been emotionally distant from him, decides to open up about his feelings. He saw his wife get warped in jealousy and resentment over Sam and Sara and feels her stubborn nature to forgive their son for choosing against her wishes took a toll on her health.

He musters the courage to engage in a heart-to-heart with Sam. He encourages him to rejoin his job and reconcile his differences with Sara. Sam, who never saw his father as a confidant, is astonished by his suggestion. He decides to make amends with Sara.

Since Sam's return, his mother's health had slowly improved. She smiled and laughed more, and became more active in her life. When she finds out that her husband suggested Sam should rejoin his job, she is undeniably sad. Deep within, she realized her over-possessiveness for her son and how she emotionally manipulated him to break up with Sara. She knows she cannot have her way this time and reluctantly lets him go.

Sam moves back and returns to his job. After a few unsuccessful tries, he gets in touch with Sara. She finally agrees to give him a second chance at their relationship. That was the only hiccup in their partnership. In a few years, they marry and are blessed with a daughter.

Let's examine the roles played out by everyone:

Sam is a straightforward man with a narcissistic personality. His parents doted on him, and this unadulterated affection resulted in over-confidence, and sometimes, cocky behaviour. At heart, he is loyal, but he tends to put all his eggs in one basket—for example, the way he overlooked his mother's needs when Sara entered his life.

He grew up with an over-emotional mother and an emotionally distant father. This led to Sam understanding the richness and the depth of emotions, and how over-expressing and under-expressing could both be detrimental. In his later years, Sam learned to balance it out. His soul's purpose was to learn humility and compassion, which is why his Higher Self kept creating situations where his ego is challenged until it broke down to reveal his real, humble self.

To master the lessons of humility and compassion, Sam's soul chose this set of parents. It was not as easy as these were soul qualities neither of his parents imbibed. This meant Sam had to learn to tap into his inner resources, trust his Higher Self and always follow the quiet voice of his intuition for it to lead him into the light.

Since neither his parents learned the lesson of true compassion themselves, Sam's Higher Self created various situations where his family members appeared as perpetrators inflicting pain or causing suffering. These childhood wounds healed when he consciously recognized the pattern and worked on correcting it. An example: his father's inattentiveness and lack of emotional availability led Sam to mistrust men, and he found it easier to make friends with the opposite sex. However, as Sam grew older, he learned to forgive his father and saw him through a lens of compassion and empathy. This ushered in immense soul growth for both.

Sam's mother played her part well as an overprotective and devoted mother who selflessly poured out her love for the two men in her life. She was a giver and sometimes got over-involved in situations, not knowing where to draw the line. Her life revolved around Sam, and due to a weak emotional connection with her husband, she sought constant attention and affection from her son.

When Sam was growing up, she was there for him through thick and thin. This had a positive reaction on Sam, who learned the lesson of respecting and valuing relationships, being there for others in times of crisis, and expressing unconditional love and loyalty. Sam also subconsciously adopted his mother's clinginess and neediness, reflected in his inability to stay away from Sara for too long. Her life lessons included learning forgiveness and moving from a vibration of resentment, jealousy, and self-hatred into love, kindness, and compassion.

Sam's father always had a stoic expression; he could not express his emotions as well as his wife. Though he prioritized his career and his work, his heart was in the right place—all he wanted to do was to support his family with a regular source of income. Growing up without a mother led him to suppress his feelings, and throughout his married life, he fought hard to overcome that pattern. His soul urged him to learn how to practice self-care, self-love, and healthy communication in relationships.

Sara was the epitome of a victim—having lost her parents at a young age led her to develop a "why me?" personality. A general sense of disempowerment led her to practice escapist tendencies, and her over-imaginative mind always created more problems than she could solve. She had to learn to face reality, feel empowered and gain control of her life. The love she felt for Sam gave her a sense of freedom. With him reciprocating the love and nurturing she so deeply craved, she felt safe and secure to step into a position of authority and power.

CASE STUDY 2 – A STORY OF ANVI AND HER HIGHER SELF

Anvi is a young girl who learns the habit of stealing from her older brother. The naïve one believes stealing is equivalent to borrowing, and for years, she continues to steal money from her father.

The father is wise and soon finds out about his daughter's bad habit, but he never catches her red-handed as his soft heart convinces him to not confront his little girl. Anvi thinks she has outsmarted her father, and once she enters her teens, she goes on to steal from her friends, even becoming brash enough to shoplift.

Anvi's Higher Self is very much aware of her doings and has often brought about rude awakenings for her to quit stealing by aligning situations and circumstances in a way that she is caught by her friends and shopkeepers. But despite getting caught in the act, Anvi bears no remorse, and her stubborn nature doesn't let her give up the fight.

Anvi's Higher Self realizes that she is not going to learn the lesson of honesty so easily, so it tweaks the situation and keeps escalating it until she has no choice. Her friends desert her and she becomes a loner. She becomes abusive and develops a bad temper. Her grades at school are at an all-time low. None of this hits Anvi as much as the news of her father's passing.

Suddenly, guilt creeps in. In all the years Anvi stole from her father, he never raised a finger at her, and the older Anvi realized that he always knew about her folly. She is overcome with shame and repentance, and this finally awakens her conscience. She turns over a new leaf, giving up the habit of stealing, lying, and being dishonest for good.

For many souls, it is a difficult journey to reach this state of awareness. We become content with the way we are, afraid to rock the boat and make amends for bad deeds we have done in the past—whether it is in this lifetime or the past ones. But some souls, like Anvi, find the light at the end of the tunnel and completely learn their lesson finally. When a life lesson is fully learned, it positively impacts our future lives too, ensuring we are strong and aware to rise above temptation when it comes knocking at the door.

Chapter 6

· · ❖ · ·

ACCESSING YOUR AKASHIC RECORDS

You may be wondering that if you consciously don't remember your past lives or the soul contract you wrote, how will you remember the exact lessons you've learned? The good news is that the soul remembers. The knowledge that a soul accumulates stays with it. It's all stored in the higher realms of Akashic Records.

The Hall of Akashic Records is a library of consciousness that is encoded in the heavenly realms. Also known as the Hall of Records or the Hall of Journals, it houses sacred books encrypted with detailed aspects of each Earthly life your soul has lived.

Every thought and every action that a soul has taken in the past, is taking in the present, or will possibly take in the future is collected in this archive of soul information. Your thoughts, words, and actions are recorded daily in the Akashic Records under your soul name. All good deeds and bad deeds are recorded under your soul name, and the collective story your soul is living is showcased karmically through these Records.

Each one of us is privy to these energetic records, and one way of accessing these is through deep meditation. Each person's records are private and secure; no one else has access to them except you and your guardian angels.

The Akashic Records can be found in the Realm to which the soul belongs. When a soul progresses or digresses spiritually, and moves to a higher or lower realm, the Akashic Records follow. They are updated every night by every soul's Higher Self when their physical body on Earth is in a deep, dreamless sleep.

The Akashic Records are located high above in the space surrounding Earth. It is protected by nonphysical beings known as Lords of the Records or the Librarians of the Records. The Records are always evolving and expanding as time infinitely continues on Earth.

So, why would we want to access our soul's Akashic Records? Reading our soul's history and the current journey we are on can help us understand what our soul's karma is. We can see all the karmic lessons we've accomplished, the lessons that are pending, and the lessons we are creating for ourselves unconsciously.

The biggest benefit of reading the Akashic Records is that the awareness you gain instantly helps deepen the connection you share with your Higher Self. You understand yourself on a deeper level, and you come closer to achieving what you had planned for your soul's journey in this present life you're living.

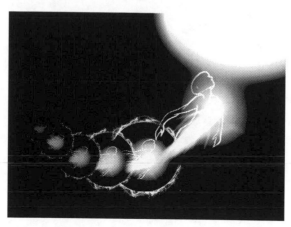

*By accessing the Akashic Records, you open the doorway to explore all
your past lives on Earth. By doing this, you can consciously awaken
your gifts and skills carried forth from your past incarnations.*

It is advisable to take advantage of this heightened awareness and hidden information so that we can accomplish our soul's mission in this lifetime. Gaining deeper knowledge about our soul's origins can also plant seeds for positive experiences in future lives.

When you are visiting your Records in the Akashic Realm, you will never see the Lords of the Records. However, you may see loved ones who have passed over or helping spirit guides if they have a message for you.

The information you receive in every visit will be limited—do not place expectations on the knowledge that comes through. Sometimes it will be felt through subtle vibrational shifts in your physical body or it could also be a sudden flash of awareness that brings insight to a question you were querying about.

This high dimension of consciousness is open for all souls to access. However, only sincere spiritual seekers will be able to cross over and stay awake through the process. Most of the time, when your soul is *consciously* trying to access the Records like we are doing in this book, your physical body will be in deep sleep and your mind in a dreamless state. This is so that the awareness or knowledge can be downloaded into your mind through a safe and secure process.

It is important to be aware of the time and space of where you are accessing the Akashic Records. It's best to do it at home in a space where you will be undisturbed for a few hours.
When you are starting, you may not receive major revelations or mind-blowing information as that will unsettle you. The journey to understand your soul's history is a slow and steady process. Just the way we cannot get through a day or 24 hours in a moment, we cannot access the information we are not ready to hear. Stick with the process and you will be rewarded.

You must learn to trust yourself and believe the information you are receiving. The more you access the Records, the more you will understand how it works. The process is akin to raising our spiritual awareness. If your Crown chakra is imbalanced or your Third Eye chakra is blocked, you may not be able to perceive the information that is coming through. Therefore, every soul needs to maintain spiritual hygiene in their life.

Since the Akashic Records update every night when we sleep, it is up to us to make the right choices and stick to a path of honesty and integrity so that we are creating a positive future in the afterlife. As Newton's third law goes, "For every action, there is an equal and opposite reaction," this is true in the Spirit Realm as well.

If you are a positive soul with an abundance of good karma, your Records will be light and white in colour. If you are a dark soul with negative karma, your Records will be heavy and black in colour. Many are a mix of both, making your Records weigh according to your karma with a grayish colour.

It is important to understand that these Records are not physical books. The Hall of Records is nothing like a physical library full of books—though it can be understood as that metaphorically. These Records are energetic, and they are bound to your soul through a silver etheric cord. It is like your own secure connection to opening the Records.

The information that comes through each visit may link to a challenge or a struggle you are currently facing. It could also be lessons yet to learn or messages related to what is happening in your life at that point. Essentially, the knowledge you receive will be healing and loving. It will help you in developing an unconditional understanding of the true nature of your being. You will understand why you are here on planet Earth, what your soul's mission is, how you can attain it, how you can overcome the obstacles standing in your way and so much more.

The knowledge that is willing to come through the Hall of Records is really astounding and can drastically improve or shift the vibration of your current life. Opening this door can bring in a shower of spiritual wisdom, helping you attain enlightenment sooner if you are ready to put in the necessary spiritual work.

The guidance you receive or the visions you experience are always meant to elevate you and raise your consciousness. The focus is always on facilitating your soul's growth in the kindest manner possible.

Your spirit guides always know the best way to help you with your challenges, and they are always watching over you to ensure you do not tread too far from your soul's plan. They will only give information that is safe, reliable, and easy for you to understand. Don't expect mysterious messages to decode or metaphysical concepts you are not ready to understand. It is important you do not compare the messages you receive with anyone else's. Your journey is unique and so is the guidance you will receive.

It is best to begin the journey by preparing your list of questions. You may not know what query will get answered, but it is better to present a long list for your Higher Self to choose from. The key to getting accurate information is by asking the right questions such as:

What do I need to know about my soul's purpose?
How do I gain more insight about…?
Do I accept all sides of myself?
What thought patterns are limiting me?
Am I being true to myself?
What life problems am I in denial about?
What messages does my Higher Self have for me?
What do I need to let go of?

These are just a few questions to get your journey started into exploring the majestic Akashic Records. Remember to always ask questions that align with your values and resonate with your beliefs.

Are you ready to explore your soul's Akashic Records? The below exercise will gently kick-start your journey into the heavenly realms.

EXERCISE 9: ACCESSING YOUR AKASHIC RECORDS

Step 1
Prayer

Step 2
Meditation

Step 3
Journaling

Step 1 – Prayer
To open your connection to the Records, let's begin with a sincere and short prayer. This sacred prayer uses high-vibrational words and phrases that create an energetic bridge to the Akashic Records.
Bring your attention to your breath, and notice how you are feeling in your body. Imagine a bright white light surrounding your body, and allow

it to settle around you, creating a bubble of healing energies. This light is nurturing and gentle. Let it wash over your physical body, cleansing away all toxins and negativity.

Now, speak aloud the following prayer:

We acknowledge the forces of light,
We ask for divine guidance and direction,
Oh lord, show us the path right,
And let us seek an ecstatic reunion,
With our Higher Selves in a higher realm.
Oh lord, help us, heal us, love us, guide us,
Unconditionally, so we have the wisdom,
To attain enlightenment, like a blossoming lotus.

Now, silently repeat the following prayer:

Help me understand (your complete legal name)'s Akashic Records in the white light of God's divinity. Please open the energetic seal so that my soul's wounds heal. Please shed pure light on my soul through the eyes of the Lords of the Records. Thank you, thank you, thank you.

Now, read aloud the following affirmation:
The Records for (your complete legal name) are now open with divine light.

Step 2 – Meditation
Sit or lie down in a comfortable position and follow the guided meditation.

PART 1: GUIDED MEDITATION (10 MINUTES)

Slowly bring your attention to your breath. Focus on breathing in the light of the Universe, and exhaling your stresses. Take a deep inhale through your nose, and exhale loudly through your mouth. Inhale, and exhale. As you breathe in, focus on bringing in the beautiful white light of the Universe, and as you exhale, you are letting go of everything you have been holding on to.

Now, when you inhale, you will hold your breath for up to 5 seconds. Inhale the light of the Universe, inhale as much as you can, and now hold. 1, 2, 3, 4, 5. Exhale loudly. Repeat this process two more times.

Now that you have connected with your breath, your mind will be feeling calmer and more centred. Let's ground our energies and connect with Mother Earth. Imagine a vibrant pink light coming out from the tips of your toes and the soles of your feet, moving out into the ground through your feet. This beautiful pink light is taking away all your negative energy that has become stuck in your body through the stresses you are feeling. You don't even have to do anything; this light is automatically taking this negative energy away from your body and back into the Earth where it recycles into new creative energy.

Take a deep inhale through your nose, and exhale through your mouth.

As the pink light heals your stresses, imagine a silver cord coming out from the bottom of your feet, moving into the Earth, and inching closer to the core of the Earth. This silver cord now begins to anchor itself to the Earth's core, establishing a strong connection between your body and the Earth. Once the cord is anchored, the energy surges back up through the deep layers of the Earth, and it comes right back into your feet.

Now, move this energy upwards to cleanse your aura. Visualize the pink light hovering around your feet to move up your ankles, your calves, your knees, and your thighs. Moving up your stomach, your chest, moving around your back, your shoulders, your neck, your throat, moving up your face, and your head. This beautiful, vibrant, radiant pink light is all around your body now.

Surrender your worries to this light. Breathe in its innocence and its lightheartedness. Feel how it feels to be completely free, alive, awakened, and relish the warmth that this pink light is giving you unconditionally.

Let this pink light work its magic on your aura and cleanse away any negative energy. Finish the meditation by chanting Om three times.

Om

Om

Om

PART 2: SILENT MEDITATION (20 MINUTES)

Continue relaxing in this condition for the next 20 minutes.

You are the Universe experiencing itself. Meditate
on what is to be happy in the here and now.

Step 3 – Journaling

Once the meditation is complete, bring out your journal and begin writing.
You can personalize the questions to suit you.

Why am I here? What am I here to do?

_____

_____

_____

_____

_____

_____

What do I need to know about my soul's purpose?

_____

_____

_____

_____

_____

_____

What messages does my Higher Self have for me?

_____

_____

_____

_____

_____

What thought patterns are limiting me?

_____

_____

_____

_____

_____

What do I need to let go of?

_____

_____

_____

_____

_____

What do I need to do more of?

_____

_____

_____

_____

How can I give back and serve with my gifts?

_____

_____

_____

_____

_____

How can I make this Earth a better world to live in?

_____

_____

_____

_____

_____

Well done! You have successfully accessed your Akashic Records. Repeat this practice with follow-up questions to get clarity on all the karmic challenges in your life. Observe signs, synchronicities, meaningful or unusual dreams, messages, insights, visions, or more from your Higher Self as it assists you in remembering who you are.

Chapter 7

· · ❖ · ·

ACTIVATING YOUR CHAKRAS

When we arrive on this planet, we come devoid of memories. The day we are born is our soul starting afresh, and as we grow, we collect positive and negative information from our surroundings. Sometimes, we gather memories, experiences, and emotions that are not so pleasant. This energy gets stuck in our physical body within our chakras.

Chakra is a Sanskrit word that translates to a "wheel". Chakras are pools of spiralling energy in the human body, and there are seven major chakras or wheels of energy that correspond with a particular body part, emotion, sound, colour, mantra, *mudra*, and vibration.

All seven chakras—Root chakra, Sacral chakra, Solar Plexus chakra, Heart chakra, Throat chakra, Third Eye chakra, and Crown chakra—are vertically located along the spine and extend upward to the crown of the head.

Each chakra emits a different frequency and resonates with a certain type of crystal. For example, the Third Eye chakra, which is located in between the eyebrows, vibes with a purple/indigo crystal, like amethyst.

The lower chakras—Root chakra, Sacral chakra, and Solar Plexus chakra—emit a denser vibration that relates to material things on the Earthly plane. The higher chakras—Heart chakra, Throat chakra, Third Eye chakra, and Crown chakra—emit a higher vibration that relates to universal consciousness in the spiritual realm.

Each chakra center spins in a clockwise direction, like a fan, emitting and receiving vibrations from the environment, day-to-day experiences, interactions with people, etc. The chakras have a sponge-like memory, and the energetic body remembers each life incident. Positive memories and healthy emotions balance the associated chakra, whereas negative memories and unhealthy emotions get stuck in the associated chakra, causing an energetic leak or an imbalance.

If the chakras are open, the vibrations are high, and we feel happy, light, and healthy. If the chakras get blocked, the vibrations are low, and we feel sick, stressed, and tired. If left unhealed, imbalanced chakras lead to low energy levels, poor lifestyle choices, and physical illness in the long term. Just the way we take care of our physical body, it is vital we take care of our emotional, mental, and spiritual bodies. Regularly checking in with our chakras can help us understand our emotional patterns and release energy that is no longer serving us.

Chakra (Sanskrit name)	Colour	Element	Location	Gland	Crystals	Planets
Root (*Muladhara*)	Red, Black	Earth	Base of spine	Adrenals	Ruby, Hematite, Agate, Garnet	Earth, Saturn
Sacral (*Svadhisthana*)	Orange	Water	Between pubic bone and navel	Ovaries, Testicles	Carnelian, Calcite, Orange Topaz, Fluorite	Jupiter
Solar Plexus (*Manipura*)	Yellow, Gold	Fire	Between navel and sternum	Pancreas	Citrine, Topaz, Amber	Mars
Heart (*Anahata*)	Green, Pink	Air	Centre of chest	Thymus	Rose Quartz, Jade, Malachite	Venus
Throat (*Vishuddha*)	Blue, Turquoise	Sound/vibration	Base of throat	Thyroid and Parathyroid	Lapis Lazuli, Turquoise, Amazonite	Mercury
Third Eye (*Ajna*)	Violet, Indigo	Light	Between the eyebrows	Pituitary	Amethyst, Purple Striped Agate, Purple Lepidolite	Sun, Moon
Crown (*Sahasrara*)	White, Silver	Thought	Top of the head	Pineal	Clear Quartz, Selenite	All stars, planets, galaxies, and Universes

Figure 3.1 The seven chakras and their respective associations.

Every day is a fresh start. We have 24 hours as an opportunity to create something new. Each morning when you wake up, you awaken to fresh opportunities, unending possibilities, and infinite new beginnings. However, human beings are creatures of habit. We choose to fill these precious moments repeating the actions we took yesterday, thinking repetitive thoughts, behaving the same way, and living on auto-pilot. We constantly get stuck in a thinking-creating-thinking cycle where we lose track of the present moment.

Our life has become a bundle of memories that we are living repeatedly. The new experiences we are creating are reminiscent of the past. In each moment, we are carrying the old into it. We need to learn to shift between different emotions and states of being to bring our attention to the here and now.

Set yourself free from your past stories and move into a space of unfettered peace and contentment, where all is well in your world. As you release toxic traits and negative habits, the blocks in your chakras will dissolve, allowing a greater flow of energy into your life.

EXERCISE 10: RELEASING NEGATIVE INFORMATION STORED IN YOUR CHAKRAS

Part 1: Visualization

Imagine you're standing in front of a big dumpster.
It's overloaded with trash, and it has a rather pungent smell that you instantly catch a whiff of.
Even though the sight isn't pleasant to the eye, you still feel implored to inch closer and go through the garbage.
You walk to the dumpster and start sifting through the stuff. As you do that, your attention moves to a sparkling crystal partly hidden inside a box.
You pick it up and marvel at its wondrous patterns that reflect playfully in the sunlight.
You put it in your pocket and continue walking on your path forward.

Life is like this big, smelly dumpster. Most of our life experiences and memories of times when we were not in control created unpleasant memories, unhealthy emotions, and negative beliefs about ourselves.

What was your life like as a child? Did you feel like you were in power, or were your parents in power? What reality did your parents create for you? Growing up, what reality did you eventually create for yourself? What are you holding on to from your childhood?

It is time to let go of garbage-like thoughts and the fowl stench it has left in their wake. The meaningful moments you fondly remember are the cherished crystals you should be safekeeping in your heart.

Let us cleanse our chakras and rinse them of all dense energies. There is no better time than now to release the stress and anxiety you have experienced along with any other unpleasant memories from the past and turn over a new leaf. Are you ready to let go of the old and start a new life story?

Part 2: Journaling

Before you begin writing, it is important to practice the visualization in step 1.
Write down the first thoughts that come to you.

What am I ready to let go of?

_____

_____

_____

_____

_____

_____

What thought patterns or emotional patterns can I release?

_____

_____

_____

_____

_____

_____

What negative beliefs about myself am I ready to transmute?

_____

_____

_____

_____

_____

_____

What or who is no longer serving me?

_____

_____

_____

_____

_____

EXERCISE 11: BALANCING YOUR CHAKRAS

Step 1
Chakra Healing Lightwork Meditation

Step 2
Body Healing and Sound Healing

Step 3
Positive Affirmations

Step 1 – Chakra Healing Lightwork Meditation
Sit or lie down in a comfortable position and follow the guided meditation.

Take a deep inhale through your nose, and exhale through your mouth.

Begin by bringing your attention to your Root chakra located at the base of the spine. This chakra is the primal energy center and it governs the basic survival needs. Imagine a ball of red light emanating from the base of your spine. This energy ball is moving around like a fan, and slowly, as you observe it, the speed starts increasing. This bright red ball of energy is now moving at a fast speed, opening, and aligning your Root chakra as appropriate.

Inhale. Exhale.

Move on to your Sacral chakra, located right below your belly button, which deals with emotions, relationships, pleasure, sexuality, and creativity. Imagine a ball of orange light circulating right below your belly. This energy ball is moving around like a fan, and slowly, as you observe it, you notice that the speed starts increasing. This bright orange ball of energy is now circulating at a fast speed, opening, and aligning your Sacral chakra as appropriate.

Inhale. Exhale.

Move on to your Solar Plexus chakra, located in your stomach area, which deals with intellect, ambition, the strength of will, personal power, individuality, self-worth, and freedom of choice. Imagine a ball of bright yellow light circulating in your stomach area. This energy ball is moving around like a fan, and slowly, as you observe it, you notice that the speed starts increasing. This yellow ball of energy is now circulating at a fast speed, opening, and aligning your Solar Plexus chakra as appropriate.

Inhale. Exhale.

Move on to your Heart chakra, located in the center of your chest, which deals with love, compassion, universal consciousness, emotional balance, and forgiveness. Visualize a ball of green light circulating in the center of your chest. This energy ball is moving around like a fan, and slowly, as you observe it, you notice that the speed starts increasing. This bright green ball of energy is now circulating at a fast speed, opening, and aligning your Heart chakra as appropriate.

Inhale. Exhale.

Move on to your Throat chakra located in the neck, which deals with communication, self-expression, creativity, and your inner voice. Imagine a ball of blue light moving around your throat area. This energy ball is moving around like a fan, and slowly, as you observe it, you notice that the speed starts increasing. This bright blue ball of energy is now circulating at a fast speed, opening, and aligning your Throat chakra as appropriate.

Inhale. Exhale.

Move on to your Third Eye chakra, located on your forehead just between the eyebrows, which deals with spiritual awareness, seeing, insight, visualization, intuition, psychic powers, and imagination. Visualize a ball of purple light coming through the center of your eyebrows. This bright purple light is stirring your third eye, allowing it to open. Just the way your eyes open in the morning when you wake up, allow your Third Eye chakra to naturally open as much as it can.

Inhale. Exhale.

Move on to the Crown chakra, located at the top of your head, which deals with spirituality, energy, pure awareness, enlightenment, fulfillment, and cosmic consciousness. Imagine a beautiful white and gold light surrounding your head, allowing you to feel connected to the Source. This white and gold light is bringing in recognition of your divinity and it makes you feel aware of the miracle of your consciousness.

Inhale. Exhale.

Finish the meditation by chanting Om three times.

Om
Om
Om

Slowly, bring your attention back to your body. Wiggle your toes, move your fingers, and come back into this present moment. When you feel ready, you can open your eyes.

Step 2 – Body Healing and Sound Healing

Practicing the seven *mudras* and chanting the specific mantra or sacred sound awakens the chakra. These hand positions signal your nervous system to slow down and your mind to relax as your attention draws to the world within. Refer to the figure below and begin practicing from the Root chakra to the Crown chakra.

Chakra Cleansing & Balancing Mudras & Mantras

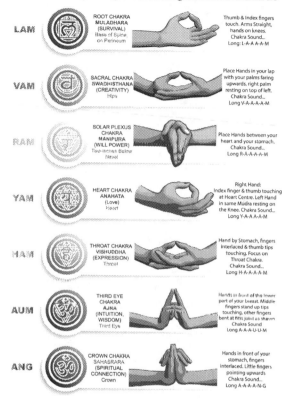

LAM		ROOT CHAKRA MULADHARA (SURVIVAL) Base of Spine, on Perineum	Thumb & Index fingers touch. Arms Straight, hands on knees. Chakra Sound... Long: L-A-A-A-M
VAM		SACRAL CHAKRA SWADHISTHANA (CREATIVITY) Hips	Place Hands in your lap with your palms faring upwards, right palm resting on top of left. Chakra Sound... Long V-A-A-A-M
RAM		SOLAR PLEXUS CHAKRA MANIPURA (WILL POWER) Two inches Below Navel	Place Hands between your heart and your stomach. Chakra Sound... Long R-A-A-A-M
YAM		HEART CHAKRA ANAHATA (Love) Heart	Right Hand: Index finger & thumb touching at Heart Centre. Left Hand in same Mudra resting on the knee. Chakra Sound... Long Y-A-A A-A-M
HAM		THROAT CHAKRA VISHUDDHA (EXPRESSION) Throat	Hand by Stomach, fingers Interlaced & thumb tips touching. Focus on Throat Chakra. Chakra Sound... Long H-A-A-A-M
AUM		THIRD EYE CHAKRA AJNA (INTUITION, WISDOM) Third Eye	Hands in front of the lower part of your breast. Middle fingers stand up tips touching, other fingers bent at first joint as shown Chakra Sound Long A-A-A-U-U-M
ANG		CROWN CHAKRA SAHASRARA (SPIRITUAL CONNECTION) Crown	Hands in front of your stomach, fingers interlaced. Little fingers pointing upwards Chakra Sound... Long A-A-A-A-N-G

*Balance your seven chakras by practicing
these mudras and ancient mantras.*

Step 3 – Positive Affirmations

Repeat these affirmations aloud to yourself in front of a mirror, preferably in the morning before starting your day.

For the Root chakra:

I am grounded and connected to Mother Nature.
I have enough material possessions.
The Earth supports all my needs.
I am safe and secure in the here and now.

For the Sacral chakra:
I respect my body and take good care of it.
I respect all relationships in my life.
I am a creative being and I take pleasure in creating.
I am a sweet soul and I create emotionally-fulfilling relationships.

For the Solar Plexus chakra:
I am in power. I am in control of myself.
My inner light shines bright.
I am confident in myself and I have strong willpower.
I have healthy self-esteem and I am a responsible being.

For the Heart chakra:
My heart is open to love. I love myself and everyone else.
My heart is like a lotus—blossoming despite muddy waters.
I am love. I am light. I forgive everyone.
I make choices that align with my heart.

For the Throat chakra:
I speak my truth easily.
I share my inner voice with the world.
I am a powerful orator.
I express how I feel.

For the Third Eye chakra:
I follow my intuition. I listen to my inner wisdom.
I now open my spiritual eye to see through illusion.
I trust myself to act on the visions in my mind's eye.
I now awaken my soul.

For the Crown chakra:
I am the Universe; the Universe is me.
I am always connected to the Source.
I am a channel of divine intelligence and wisdom.

I invite cosmic consciousness to flow through me.

10 Ways to Activate Latent Energies in Your Chakras

1. Become conscious of the negative stories you are telling yourself and others, and replace them with encouraging self-talk.
2. Recognize the areas where you are bringing up resistance to change.
3. Learn to experience uncomfortable feelings here and now to ensure they are not suppressed in the body.
4. Cut ties with pessimistic friends and break up toxic relationships.
5. Donate possessions that no longer bring you joy.
6. Detox your diet to release toxins from your body.
7. Break away from negative thought patterns and bad habits by replacing them with positive affirmations.
8. Stop controlling your future and courageously surrender to the flow of life.
9. Start practicing present-moment awareness by becoming aware of your breath to experience every minute fully.
10. Learn to forgive those who have wronged you to let go of anger and resentment.

Chapter 8

...❖...

ESTABLISHING A MINDFULNESS PRACTICE

Who are you? Are you this physical body or are you a soul?

Your spiritual journey begins by asking yourself this question.

By now, you theoretically understand that you are a manifestation of God living in a physical form. *Atman* is *Brahma*. You are the Universe experiencing itself. We are all interconnected beings.

However, Earth is a denser plane and as humans, we have collected karma over past births that we are still balancing out with fellow soul mates. To understand those karmic patterns and to clear them, a spiritual seeker has to dive deeper within to do a self-analysis through meditation and deep introspection.

In this age of social media where instant gratification rules over common sense, we have become so distracted by our five senses that sitting in quiet contemplation is the medicine we must self-administer for our soul to recover.

Self-evaluation only happens when you look at yourself objectively and contemplate your thoughts and actions. When you become aware of your actions and you observe the reactions they are causing, you will conclude whether that action was good or not. Dependent on your action, it will be easy for you to discern the quality and vibration of your soul. Good actions create good karma and poor actions create bad karma.

Research shows that the human mind thinks around 60,000 thoughts every day. Out of all these thoughts, some are positive but most are negative. If the mind is treated to good thoughts and positive experiences in your environment, it creates a vibrational shift within. A well-cultivated mind can blossom like flowers. Similarly, a mind poisoned with negative thoughts can cause negative feelings to fester in the heart, symbolized by withering and decaying flowers.

Every thought you think and every action you take is stored in the Akashic Records, so become self-conscious of the happenings in your inner landscape. During the day, the mind gets busy, so create a nighttime routine of reviewing your daily actions before you sleep. Maintaining a journal where you jot down your thoughts and express gratitude will immensely strengthen your spiritual journey and will help unlock the gates to enlightenment.

The end goal is to overcome the negative information that has seeped into our minds from external sources and replace it with positive information about love and light. Practicing mindful meditation allows you to become aware of your thought patterns and your emotions. Your thoughts influence your emotions, so always keep checking in with yourself to see how you are feeling. If you are feeling good, it means you are thinking positive thoughts. If you are feeling bad, then you are stuck in negative thinking. Meditation helps bring awareness to these thought patterns and by simply shedding light on them, the negative thoughts dissolve into nothingness.

Your mind is influenced by your environment and the people you surround yourself with. At the same time, the images you visualize in your mind manifest in your external reality. So, paying close attention to the vibration of thoughts in your mind through meditation will help you analyze yourself and your soul standing.

Meditation helps you to start separating yourself from your thoughts by realizing that thoughts are mental programs running on auto-pilot mode and therefore are not you. In other words, you are not your thoughts. You are the soul, residing in the Third Eye chakra. You are the observer, objectively watching your physical body and mind's actions with detachment. Practicing mindfulness also opens your Heart chakra and brings universal love and kindness into your life. You become kinder to the people in your life because you realize, we are all one.

Another reason to meditate is that it induces relaxed brain waves. When your mind slows down, your altered brain waves produce theta and alpha waves which are known to boost creativity and enhance problem-solving abilities. Establishing a daily meditation practice is a sure-shot way to ensure a healthy brain in the long term.

As you settle down to meditate, begin by affirming in your mind that you are perfectly safe wherever you are in this moment right now and that no harm can come to you. As you feel comfortable in your environment, you become comfortable in your internal environment as well. As the noise fades away and distractions come to a standstill, your subconscious mind opens to reveal the truth of your soul.

As within, so without. What is inside is what is outside. Your life reflects your inner reality and your thoughts are shaping your everyday existence. Look at all the areas in your life—from your health to your relationships and career—and honestly assess whether you are content with where you are at. Look at all the areas you do not want to look at as well. For example, if you are avoiding or ignoring doing something like going to the gym as you had told yourself you would, reflect on why that is in your meditation practice and allow your subconscious mind to guide you.

When you go within, you create space for major healing to happen. When you close your eyes and tune in to your intuition, you connect with the all-knowing guidance that shows you a higher perspective of why you are going through the current karmic challenges in your life.

Self-evaluation creates transparency between your soul and your ego. You become honest with yourself and learn to let go of bad habits like excessive drinking, smoking, eating, sleeping, or overthinking. You realize that your actions are harming or deterring your soul's growth and change happens automatically. Change begins within and then reflects in the external realm.

The best thing about meditation is that it is free. All we must do is be in the flow of existence and allow every moment to unfold naturally without expecting a certain outcome or holding on to a preferred version of reality. The key is to surrender and accept what the Universe puts in your path. Anything that does not align with your Higher Self's vision of your life will not work out anyway, so let it go now.

With a daily mindfulness practice, you learn to trust the voice within and you know you will never stray from your soul's purpose. The goal of meditation is to be here now and experience the joy of being alive.

EXERCISE 12: CONNECTING WITH YOUR HIGHER SELF

Before you begin writing, sit in a comfortable position, close your eyes, and take a deep breath.
Inhale, exhale.
Now, ground yourself by visualizing a bright white light surrounding your body. This powerful healing light cleanses and refreshes you completely.
Upon opening your eyes, write down the first thoughts that come to you.

What is my soul here to achieve?

_____
_____
_____
_____
_____
_____

How can I accomplish my dreams?

_____
_____
_____
_____
_____
_____

How can my soul serve?

_____
_____
_____
_____
_____
_____

What guidance do I need at this moment right now?

_____
_____
_____
_____
_____
_____

Connecting with your Higher Self is just like calling someone using your phone. First, you dial the number or find their contact and then press the call button. Then, you wait for them to answer. Similarly, when we close our eyes to meditate and visualize the white light around us, we are dialling into the frequency of our Higher Self. Then, we wait for a response. Sometimes, the response will be a stream of words, vivid visions, or strong feelings, which is why it is best to write down the messages you are receiving lest you forget them. The way our Higher Self connects with us will differ for every soul, but the way we contact our Higher Self is the same. Repeat the above method for any question you may have for your Higher Self and be patient with how you receive the answers.

3 WAYS TO DEAL WITH RESISTANCE TO CHANGE

As you connect with your Higher Self, you may experience resistance coming up. This happens when the ego is in fear. You must surrender to your Higher Self and allow the process to unfold by itself.

1. Overcoming procrastination
Do you think you are too lazy to meditate? If you think you are lazy, you will feel lazy. That is just how powerful words and their associations are. Understand where your patterns of laziness are stemming from. Did an authority figure in your life call you lazy? Did you procrastinate as a child? Are you afraid of what success looks like? What is stopping you? Is anyone holding you back?

2. Centering yourself in the present
Replace "I'll do it tomorrow" with "I'll do it now". As Eckhart Tolle rightly points out in his book, *The Power of Now*, the seed of real action lies dormant in every present moment. Every second we spend breathing can be mindful.
Learn to act in the NOW. There is nothing more powerful than this present moment. Being aware and awake in every moment will align your consciousness to what is important for yourself, and once you move over the initial bump, you will realize it is smooth sailing after that.
What can you do right now to improve your situation?

3. Understanding your 'why'

Just the way setting an intention before you begin any practice helps you align the outcome in your favour, similarly, understanding why you want to connect with your Higher Self will help you remove any resistance.

Go deeper within to understand what is stopping you from achieving your goals and remove the veil of distraction.

Part 3

Chapter 9

· · ❖ · ·

STRENGTHENING YOUR AURA FOR SELF-PROTECTION

Planet Earth is currently going through a major shift.

We are living in the age of *Kali Yuga*, the age of darkness and selfishness where human beings are fighting with each other—and ultimately with themselves. Dark energies are waging a war against light forces. There is so much pain and suffering on Earth, and these low vibrations have made Mother Earth heavy with bad karmic actions.

Lightworkers, angelic beings, saints, and protectors of the Earth are watching over as Earth cleanses itself of negative forces and energies. Each soul has double protection—their subconscious mind and their spirit guide—but they also have free will, which means they can choose to follow the right path or the one that will lead them astray.

Most souls are asleep, submerged in dark energies of anxiety, depression, anger, jealousy, shame, and guilt. These negative emotions are a result of negative thoughts, and the pattern becomes a vicious cycle difficult to break out of. Meanwhile, there are groups of souls leading meditations and facilitating mass healing for everyone's benefit, including the planet.

The forces of light are working hard to fight evil. This also applies to the positive and negative thoughts or emotions within ourselves. We all have a dark side, or as Carl Jung called it, a shadow self. This is the side of us that houses repressed emotions and unexpressed energy that you hide from the world. Its opposite is the good side, the light self, which sees universality and love as its guiding factors.

On Earth, we have the free will to choose our path—the good side or the evil side. If you choose the path of positive thinking, universal love, kindness, peace, harmony, and charity, you will rise higher spiritually. If you choose the dark side and fall into patterns of negative thinking, hurting or harming others, cheating, lying, or deceiving others, you will fall into lower realms. You cannot do things the wrong way and then expect them to work out. You must do things the right way. You must face your fears and your karmic challenges head-on and rise toward the light. Even if you fall spiritually, acknowledge your mistakes, and then move on from anything that no longer serves your soul's purpose.

Every soul must learn to protect themselves and deflect negative energies, especially sensitive souls who are empaths and innocent souls who easily trust everyone. If you do not protect your energy by establishing strong boundaries, you will find yourself attracting people who are energy vampires, manipulative narcissists, or of a lower vibrational field that will bring you down leaving you tired, drained, and exhausted. They will want to control you, abuse you, take advantage of you, and make you do things you do not want to do. You must learn to say no and draw the line somewhere.

Therefore it is important to become mindful of the vibrations you are letting into your auric field. Your aura is taking on more energy from your environment than you are aware of. The big question is whether that energy is positive or negative.
The collective energy of the Earth is currently thriving on fear. The most debilitating aspect of living in fear is how it makes you think you are so small and that you cannot achieve anything in your life because something

terrible happened to you in the past. This victim mentality reflects your shadow self expressing itself. Learn to disassociate from any past stories that are limiting you. Forgive your parents for all past hurts. Let go of human beings and human stuff bringing you negativity. This moment is a fresh new start. Focus on your soul and the inner voice within you that will be your compass to find positive energies.

Be the change you wish to see. Be a good soul. Be a positive influence in this world. We need your light, and this light is always burning inside of you. Start sharing your light because it is going to help others come out towards the light and embrace all that there is within them.

ARE YOU AN EMPATH?

An empath is someone who can intuitively understand the feelings and emotions of people around them. You feel deeply for every human being, especially sick kids, and older people, and you desire to help them heal. You want to make the world a better place by raising its vibrations and spreading love and light.

Empaths are naturally sensitive beings, and they may be an introvert in their younger years, but an ambivert in their mature days.

Being an empath is a gift. However, if you do not cleanse your energy field, you can unconsciously start taking on people's pain and negative emotions, which becomes a burden. Your aura gathers debris and you start attracting low-vibrational people and events. The chakras become imbalanced, and the Third Eye and Crown chakras become overactive. You have to purify your aura, ground yourself, cleanse your energies, and connect with Mother Earth and the Source to keep your shield strong.

7 SIGNS AND TRAITS OF AN EMPATH

Do you feel the energies of a room as soon as you walk in?
Do you feel you can deeply understand and resonate with someone's pain?
Do you find yourself going through intense, indescribable feelings?

If you answered yes to at least one question, you could be an empath.

1. You can feel people's emotions
Whether it is a friend or a family member who is going through a difficult period, you can sense how they are energetically feeling—no matter how close or physically distant they are from you.

2. You take on people's energies
Empaths tend to pick up people's vibrations. When people around you are happy, you will reflect their high energies. But if they are feeling low vibrational feelings of shame, guilt, anger, or pain, then you will soak in their energies like a sponge. This may lead you to feel anxious or a little bit on edge. Practice grounding exercises and regularly cleanse your chakras to keep your energy clean.

3. You attract energy vampires
If you are an empath, you will notice that people will feel attracted to you like a moth to a flame. Some can have a negative impact on you, cause you to feel drained, and try to feed off your light and positivity. Maintaining healthy boundaries and ensuring you regularly clear your energies can help keep distance between you and them.

4. Strangers find you friendly and approachable
You may find a random stranger on a bus smiling at you or kindly offering you a seat. When empaths vibrate at the highest frequency possible, they radiate light and energy that others can feel. This makes others feel at ease, which is why you may find strangers approaching you for random reasons.

5. Your intuition is accurate

You connect to your inner self, and you trust your gut feeling. Whenever you feel like something is going to happen, it usually happens. You could have premonitions about people or places as well.

6. You feel drawn to help people

Children, the elderly, and the differently-abled have your attention. You feel their pain, you understand their suffering and you do your best to help them in any way possible. You could be into volunteering as well.

7. You can read people's auras

When you are chatting with someone, you are engaging with that person's aura, not their mind or ego. Their aura tells you things about them that they may not personally reveal to you. You could even build a telepathic bond with them if they are an empath as well.

HOW TO PROTECT YOUR ENERGY FROM BAD VIBES

You may not be aware of the influence people, places, and things have on you. It is subtle, but it's present. Some influences are positive, while others are not. Protecting yourself from people's energies will help you deflect bad vibes and keep your aura clean and light.

Sometimes, people can create emotional muck around your aura that can block your chakras and tarnish your self-image. Perhaps you unconsciously attract energy suckers who keep calling or texting you. Or maybe some habit from your past is following you, and you have not been able to let it go. The first step is to detox your life of all the pessimistic people or toxic habits that are pulling you down. You need to surround yourself with positive people who empower you and lift you and swap bad habits with good ones. If you encounter someone rude or mean, remember that it is not their intention to be so. They can only express a vibe they resonate with, and you do not have to take anything personally. What people think of you and say about you should not affect you at all. Other people do not matter. Only you matter, and right now, you have so much freedom to express yourself the way you want, so be at peace. Make a list of who/what is positively impacting your life, and focus on enhancing your connection with them/it.

Don't chase anybody. Chasing people pushes them away, and they will come chasing after you once you give up. By then, you would probably be over them. If someone is not interested in being with you, just let them go and move on to make space for someone new. Since we are living in *Kali Yuga*, we are bound to come across people who will bring us down. Do not get stuck with people who are shaming you, insulting you, or making you feel bad about yourself.

You deserve to feel safe and secure. You are not a victim in life. You have a purpose for being here. The external reality that you have created so far is a mere reflection of what is going on within, and what your karma for this life is. You may have been through a lot, but it's all in the past. You are here now, and all is well at this very moment. So, be in a state of complete security and tranquillity right now.

7 WAYS TO CLEANSE YOUR ENERGY FIELD AND RAISE YOUR VIBRATIONS

1. Crystals

Crystals are structured forms of molecules or atoms that emit different frequencies. Crystals are used for manifesting certain outcomes, relaxing, and rejuvenating, as well as for protection and healing purposes.

I wear crystal bracelets, crystal earrings, and crystal pendant necklaces that I handcraft myself to protect me and keep me grounded. Crystal jewellery works like an amulet—it connects with your auric field and gives out a high vibration to elevate your frequencies. You can also set an intention to a crystal to manifest your desires.

If you like wearing jewellery, you can wear tourmaline, labradorite, obsidian, bronzite, smoky quartz, selenite, or amethyst to block negative energies and protect yourself from people's low vibrations. Another option is creating a crystal grid at your home or workplace to keep your aura clear and clean. Place four crystals of clear quartz in a square and one rose quartz crystal in the center. This will keep you safe and protected from harm.

2. Lightwork visualization

Imagining yourself bathing in beautiful rays of violet light helps boost your aura. It is akin to having a shield so strong that nothing can penetrate it. To activate this field, simply close your eyes, and imagine a bubble of violet light surrounding your body, from the soles of your feet to the crown of your head. Feel yourself connecting to the Source and fill yourself up with free-flowing positive energy. Once complete, gently flutter your eyes open and move your body to integrate the lightwork.

3. Positive affirmations

Scientific studies show that positive thinking reduces anxiety, increases happy emotions, and boosts your immune system. Positive thinking rewires your brain by changing its structure and function. This process is neuroplasticity.

You can practice the chakra affirmations listed in chapter 7 or you can write down your affirmations for a personal touch. To begin, write down "I am enough" and stick it up in front of a mirror so you can affirm it every day.

4. Colour therapy

Each colour emits a different energy, and wearing a certain shade can uplift your mood or instill a sense of inner peace. Allow your intuition to guide you while picking a colour.

Colour	Spiritual Meanings
Red	Increases energy, improves vitality, brings movement
Orange	Boosts happiness, sweetens your disposition, attracts relationships
Yellow	Builds personal power, exudes joy, attracts money
Green	Opens the Heart chakra, balances emotions, brings harmony
Blue	Improves communication, releases stress, aids relaxation
Violet	Opens the Third Eye chakra, connects to the divine, channels wisdom
White	Ushers in clarity and peace, gives out universal love
Black	Protects the aura, neutralizes negative energy, deflects unwanted thoughts

Figure 4.1 The spiritual meanings of colours.

5. Space clearing

You can also protect yourself by protecting your house. Your home is an extension of you and your space reflects who you are as a person. Right from the colours on the walls to the home decor, every detail displays your personality. Home always denotes comfort. Add an extra level of protection around you by blessing your house with drops of salt water, cleaning all corners, burning incense, sage, or holy wood like Palo Santo, and placing powerful crystals like tourmaline or obsidian at your doorstep. You can also decorate your space in a minimal style to ensure clutter-free surroundings bring clarity.

6. Connecting with your Third Eye chakra

Tuning into your intuition by opening your spiritual eye is a great tool to utilize when you want to double up your self-protection. Rub both your hands together and feel the warm energy gather in between your palms. Now, direct this energy to your Third Eye chakra by placing your hands in a prayer position and raising them to the center of the forehead. Be open to receiving whatever guidance comes through. This technique helps enhance your psychic skills as well.

7. Cutting etheric cords

Etheric cords are energetic connections formed between souls. Some cords are positive and carry good intentions back and forth between the people connected. Other negative cords feed off each other and drain each other's energy. Ask your Higher Self to guide you as to whether a connection shares a positive or a negative cord.

To release a negative connection or to clear your auric field of all etheric cords, visualize a massive sword circling your body at lightning speed, starting at the top of your head and moving down until it reaches under the base of your feet. This sword cuts through all attached cords, cleansing and clearing your energy field, and restoring it to optimal health.

Chapter 10

·· ❖ ··

NOURISHING YOUR MIND, BODY, AND SOUL

There is an inner peace that lives within you. You are not aware of it, but it exists. It is always there, when the external circumstances seem awry, or when all seems like a lull before the deadly storm. This inner stillness exists.

This phase comes after you have been meditating, journaling, and reflecting for at least a few weeks or a few months.

By now, you must have removed toxic things from your life, or are in the process of moving on from them. You are consciously cleansing your days and your diet, and you make it a point to spread good vibrations through positive actions. Once you start making positive changes in yourself, your external world will reflect them. Order and structure bring about clarity and balance.

At this stage, you are ready to surrender and accept everything *as is*. No matter what is happening on the outside, you are still going to be at peace.

There could still be negative influences challenging you, but they are minor. You can easily ignore it. Most of your life is guided by positive thoughts and actions.

When you attain this inner peace within you, you will see yourself as a divine being living on Earth to fulfill a purpose. You are aware that you are one with the creator of this Universe. You are one with the Source. You are one with God. You are one with this higher power, whatever you choose to call it.

Now you can taste the sweet nectar of your spiritual awakening.

Life is eternal and ever-flowing, just like a river. Every day, you are flowing as well, and there are crests and troughs in the journey. You go through happiness and sadness, and eventually, you reach a point where you have equanimity in every action, word, or thought.

As you realize that you are one with the Universe, you will see everyone around you as a reflection of that divinity. We are all connected like a constellation of stars.

Now, you can start to live your life from this higher awareness. When interacting with others, you respect them, you are kind, compassionate, and graceful because that is how you are with yourself.

Giving is the secret to happiness. Selfless service is the best virtue to embrace. The more you give others, the more you get back. So, start giving more. Become this benevolent being who gives with an open heart and without any expectations.

There are so many children and people in need. Volunteer at a charity. Donate to a humanitarian cause. Practice compassionate living. Be kind to a stranger. Devote your time to teaching. Be generous, for the more you give, the more you get in return. It does not matter if you donate your money, time, or clothes. It is all energy. The cycle of giving and receiving keeps recycling this energy, creating an ever-lasting exchange of it.

Giving back to Mother Earth is equally beneficial. Take care of the environment by not littering and do your bit to avoid single-use plastics. Build a connection with the Earth through gardening. Make your vegetable garden in the backyard, or plant flowers or herbs and watch them grow. Whatever seeds you put into the soil, they grow. Your mind is the same, so plant seeds of positivity!

EXERCISE 13: UNDERSTANDING YOUR SPIRITUAL JOURNEY

Close your eyes and take a deep breath. Visualize white light surrounding your body. Surrender and relax in this healing light.

Upon opening your eyes, write down the first thoughts that come to you.

What areas of my life are the most important to me?

_____

_____

_____

_____

_____

_____

What aspects of these areas matter to me the most?

_____

_____

_____

_____

_____

What life goals would I set by these values?

_____

_____

_____

_____

_____

_____

What does my ideal life look like?

_____

_____

_____

_____

_____

_____

Where do I see myself in the next 5 years?

_____

_____

_____

_____

_____

_____

EXERCISE 14: PRACTICING THE LAW OF ATTRACTION

Create a vision board with the goals that you want to manifest in the next 5 years. Designing a vision board helps the thinking and feeling parts of the brain to interact and express their understanding of your collective needs and desires.

Begin by taking a few days to gather as many images as you can that reflect what you want in your physical life, your emotional life, and your spiritual life. Once you collect the images, start by arranging the most important elements that you need right now in the center and then work your way outwards.

Put it in a place where you can see it every day. You can also create a digital vision board by saving screenshots of photos in your phone's gallery.

This year, I am manifesting:

_____

_____

_____

_____

_____

_____

EXERCISE 15: PRACTICING VISUALIZATION TECHNIQUES

Take about 5 minutes in the morning or at night before you go to sleep to look at your vision board. Close your eyes and envision your new life. Feel the way you would when all your dreams come true. Feel the joy and be grateful for it as if it has already happened!

This visualization technique reminds you of your contract with the Universe to attract these things into your life. This is a mental Universe; your thoughts carry energy that produces tangible results. Practice this spiritual commitment every day and watch your dreams manifest in your life.

Chapter 11

$$\cdots \Diamond \cdots$$

RECOGNIZING EVERYTHING
IS TEMPORARY

Attaining inner peace and maintaining it brings about an acceptance and understanding that nothing is permanent on Earth. Existence is temporary. An enlightened being knows that everything is an illusion on this 3D plane.

Can you recognize who you really are? You are a soul having a worldly experience through a physical body. Give up this attachment to yourself and your ego, and give up attachment to this material world.
Do you think you can hold on to your phone, your clothes, or your belongings? The truth is that none of this is real. You can see it, but it is not real. What you cannot see, but can feel, is real.

Material possessions and belongings are all created for our use in the here and now. In the spirit realm, none of these things matter.

Turn attachment into detachment. Let everything be. *Let it all go.* Why are we running after people and material possessions? Why are we not chasing the inner light within all of us, eternal in all its glory? What is supposed to come into your soul's path will come regardless.

Most of us are either reliving our past or worrying about what will happen in the future. Why not forgive the past and let life unfold the way it is supposed to? Give up control of how life should be and live it the way it is. Do not judge your path; sometimes we choose a solitary journey, but the destination is the same.

Everything that has happened to you had a deep meaning and reason behind it. From a higher perspective, your everyday struggles are temporary in nature. The only permanent aspect that matters is your soul's growth, and this cannot happen without tough times. So, appreciate difficulties, obstacles, and challenges. Tough times did not come to stay—they eventually pass. It is your destiny to overcome them!

Have faith. You are exactly where you are supposed to be. Trust the process and keep going. Stay present in every moment. Be mindful, be grateful, and believe that things will work out.
We are not going to be here forever. We all come with an expiry date, and so does everything around us. So, learn to enjoy the transient nature of life. Only your soul is going to live forever.
Life is always flowing; there is no beginning or end. There is only an ever-lasting Now. Remembering this secret will give you eternal happiness.

HOW TO SING YOUR SOUL SONG

1. Do what makes you feel good.
2. Listen to your heart.
3. Spend time by yourself.
4. Introspect and go within.
5. Practice what you are good at.
6. Love yourself.
7. Spread joy and positivity.
8. Smile more.

9. Live in the present moment.
10. Forgive yourself and be at peace.

EVERYDAY HABITS THAT DRAIN YOUR ENERGY

Our future is the sum of our past and present actions. If you take the same actions every day, you limit your growth. What is more, if those actions are draining your energy, then you are going to wake up the next day feeling listless, tired, and mentally exhausted. You are going to go about your day like a rote routine, and there is not going to be any room for creativity.

Make your tomorrow better with conscious actions that *do not* drain your energy. Below are 6 habits that you must slowly start breaking away from…

1. Playing the victim card

Step one of personal development is recognizing that all of us, in many ways victimize ourselves. We pity ourselves, and we think others are out to get us. The reality is that the people we think are our perpetrators are victims themselves! It's an endless circle, one that can only be broken by taking our power back and realizing that we are creators manifesting our life situations through thoughts.

2. Taking things personally

Perhaps someone passed a disparaging remark or criticized you for no reason. Bless them and forgive them. Remember, how you feel is in your control. So, choose to feel good and think positively.

3. Over-stressing, over-thinking, and over-worrying

How often have you stayed awake at night wondering if everything will turn out okay? We hold on to our intentions and desires so much that we end up sabotaging them ourselves. Practicing surrender can help you ease up, relax, and let go of what is not in your control.

4. Sleeping late and waking up late

The age-old adage, "Early to bed and early to rise, makes a man healthy, wealthy, and wise" holds veracity, and science proves it. Sleeping early reduces the risk of diseases, ensures better sleep quality, improves memory and productivity, strengthens the immune system, and overall, gives you a feeling of happiness.

5. Fueling drama

If someone creates a dramatic scene, do not react. How you feel is in your control. If you feel angry, allow yourself to cool down, and move on from creating a dramatic scene. Your life is sacred, and people who do not respect your boundaries do not deserve your energy.

6. Complaining and gossiping

Maybe your boss is always critical of your work. Or, your neighbour broke up with her boyfriend in the corridor and you heard everything.

Is it necessary to re-share the story with family, friends, or co-workers? Become firm with yourself. The world has enough negativity, why do you want to be a part of it? Replace the need to complain or gossip with expressing gratitude for the little things you have. This will bring more abundance and prosperity into your life.

5 TIPS TO TRANSFORM YOUR LIFE

1. Journal about your day before hitting the bed

This is one of the most important rituals I have consistently kept up with for the last few years. Every night before sleeping, I write everything in my diary that transpired in my day, right from the time I woke up. I write the good and the bad, and let it all out, without any filter.

Empaths are more likely to feel drained out as the day ends. This is because throughout the day you have picked up on emotions and feelings from others. It is important to come back into a state of balance, and that can only happen when you self-reflect.

This simple yet powerful exercise is effective for two reasons: 1) It helps you study your emotional and mental health over time, which boosts your personal growth. 2) It helps you sleep better as you are essentially emptying your mind onto paper before you doze off.

2. Meditate before starting your day

When we wake up, we are waking up from a peaceful and restful state of being. As we go about with our day, our minds and our senses become flooded with perturbed emotions and unending distractions. If you start your day on a balanced note, you will find it easier to practice present-moment awareness when difficult times and challenges come up. You will effortlessly be able to navigate through those rough waters, thanks to the deep powers of meditation.

*Align your chakras and strengthen your aura by
building a daily meditation practice.*

3. Create emotional boundaries

This one took me a while to master but I cannot emphasize how crucial this is to inculcate in your life. The reality is that this is a selfish world we are living in, and everyone is just fending for themselves. This thought feels pessimistic to an eternal optimist like me, but this is a harsh reality I have learned with time and experience.

If you are always giving, you will realize that you are attracting people who are only interested in taking. This can create a toxic imbalance. That is why it is important to have emotional boundaries to protect you. How do you do that? By setting simple intentions. By knowing what your triggers are, recognizing red flags, and not allowing any other person to affect your energy.

4. Say no, loudly and proudly

Two letters. One word. NO.

A side-effect of being an eternal optimist is that I always said yes to everything that people wanted to do, and seldom to what I wanted to do. It took me a very long time to accept that it is okay to say, "No, I'm not comfortable doing that."

Learning to say no strengthens your willpower (which connects to your Solar Plexus chakra); it empowers you and shows others that you are worthy.

5. Detox, cleanse, repeat

Detox your body, your mind, and your life, one day at a time. Take a break from drinking alcohol or smoking. Refrain from eating fast food or outside food for a few days. Give social media a break. Do it for your physical and mental health, and emotional well-being. The longer you detox, the stronger you become.

Chapter 12

$$\cdots \diamondsuit \cdots$$

RESPECTING DEATH AND
THE AFTERLIFE

One day, this will end. Everything is temporary. This body is a rental, too. Nothing lasts forever—that relationship you thought would stay forever fades away; friends come and go; you outgrow jobs; you leave your old city behind and start anew.

Embrace endings. Embrace new beginnings. Embrace the cycle of life. You were born. You will die. There is no escaping death. What we can do is surrender to it.

The real question is, do you want to be reborn again? Seek salvation in the present moment. The only permanent aspect is your soul. Liberate your soul from karma through sincere spiritual seeking.

Ancient Egyptians recognized death as the gateway to eternity. Tibetan Buddhist monks recited chants for the dying souls from *Bardo Thodol*, the Book of the Dead, to guide them through posthumous realities.

In our culture, we fear death. However, we can learn to accept death as our great teacher. Death does not judge; it treats all beings equally.

Souls who have passed over to the spirit realm can send signs and messages to their loved ones. This can manifest as a presence you feel around your body, seeing a white feather, dreaming vivid visions, and more.

My first brush with death was when my grandfather, or *Dadaji* as we called him, passed over to the spiritual realm when I was 13 years old (interestingly, 13 is the number associated with death and endings in Tarot and Numerology). A few weeks before his soul departed, he had just quit his day job as the principal of a school, and his days were emptier than ever. My mom confided in me that ever since he lost his wife to cancer, *Dadaji* had been a bit withdrawn. I never got to meet my grandmother. Sadly, she had already left her body by the time I was born. I am sure *Dadaji* longed to reunite with her and chose to depart at that godly hour. As I was the youngest, I could not come to terms with the events that had transpired. *Dadaji* was in good health; he would go out for a walk every day but a few days before he passed, he suffered from a heart attack. My parents rushed him to the hospital the next day. He never came back. He passed away in the hospital 8 days after my 13th birthday. I was devastated and astonished unbelievably that *Dadaji* was gone forever. I tried to show I was unaffected, but all I was trying to do was escape reality. As time went by, I went through a whole transformation. I changed as a person. I dropped my bad habits, and I somehow felt cleansed.

THE IN-BETWEEN STATES

Moments before your heart stops and your body dies, your soul recognizes that it is time to leave the body. It moves up from the body and floats in the air, watching down and observing. It feels weightless and light, and there is a glow around it.

A bright white light appears, and your soul is drawn to it. This sensation is like feeling sucked into a tunnel of white light. This light guides you back home to the Source.

The last emotion you leave Earth with is the most important as it influences your afterlife. Your last thought is so important, so leave with peace. When you are leaving your body, if your soul exits from your Crown chakra, your awareness will be much more heightened in the afterlife. If you leave from lower chakras, it shows your soul is attached to the Earthly realm.

The cause of death plays a big role in deciding your afterlife experience. If the physical body suffered a traumatic blow from an external force, died in an unfortunate accident, is murdered before its time, or for any other reason that did not intentionally cause self-harm, the soul can be very disturbed. In this case, the soul is still attached to the physical body and could be in a place of mourning. The soul may choose to stay in the Earthly realm, watching over the physical body, not realizing that its identity now is of a soul with no body.

THE SPIRIT REALM

This is where you meet your spirit guides, guardian angels, ancestors, and soul mates who previously passed over to that realm.

You all get together and the theme is to reconnect and celebrate having completed your mission on Earth. Then, you and your guides go to the Hall of Akashic Records where you start replaying your recent life on Earth.

Each scene plays out like a movie. You go through all your actions—selfish and selfless—and the good ones are rewarded with ascension, while the negative ones serve as learning lessons. Your soul is judging your ego's behaviour, reactions, temperament, and habits. Your soul's growth is determined by how positive the consequences of your ego's actions were.

All your relationships and friendships are studied with great attention to detail. Your actions, intentions, and motivations are judged. From this higher perspective, your soul now has knowledge about hidden thoughts, secrets, and unsaid words that others did not communicate. This helps you understand why someone behaved a certain way, why they did what they did, and why you met them in the first place.

In this realm, your soul has increased awareness that can connect with other souls. Your soul remembers the karmic contracts you undertook with all these souls you met on Earth and this deeper knowledge brings heightened awareness, peace, and harmony.

Your soul also studies how much of your pre-decided plan you were able to action and ground into reality on Earth. For most souls, it is a surprise how differently their life played out while living on Earth as compared to the pre-decided plan. It is quite common for souls to disconnect from the Source, which is when they start feeling lost and unsure about what they are supposed to be doing in life. That is when misled souls enter darkness and despair, where they are more likely to make poor decisions and ill choices that result in more ignorance. When such souls repeatedly take wrong actions and keep indulging in bad habits, they are avoiding their lessons. Ignorance is blissful, and some souls spend years and years stuck in the same cycle of wrongdoing. When this happens and the soul does not learn the lesson it intended to master, it will have to come back to Earth with a new ego identity.

If your soul has not learned to master the lessons you need to learn, you will have no choice but to reincarnate again to clear out your soul's karma. You will come back to Earth in a new body with no memory of who you were before, when or where you were previously born, or what your soul's plan was in the last birth. We are born with a clean slate so we can learn to master our soul's lessons that will usher in the much-needed growth that will allow our souls to move up the scale of light and vibration. Your next life will either maintain the same pace as the past life, or it will be a shade darker with more challenging circumstances so that your soul learns the lesson. This will teach your soul to not make the same mistakes. Sometimes, some souls keep partaking in bad deeds because they have become comfortable with it. It keeps getting difficult with each life until the lesson is complete.

Once your soul and your guides have explored your recent life, you start charting out a path for your next lifetime. You have access to all your past lives in the Hall of Akashic Records and the knowledge accumulated through those lifetimes is available, too. You spend time studying your past lives, the lessons learned, and the growth gained, and you evaluate the steps and actions you need to take in a physical form to help your soul ascend to higher levels of being.

This plan is a continuation of the soul's journey through consciousness. The storyline could vastly differ from the plan it created for itself in a previous life, or it could be in the same vein. In each life, the soul sets challenges to endure and overcome, with growth serving as the goal. However, the trials could differ for every soul.

While you are in the spirit realm, you are resting and recharging as you are going through old lifetimes. You are studying your growth, seeing where you are lacking, and how ascended souls are excelling. You can also look at soul mates alive on Earth and see how they are doing. If they need help, you can send them signs and messages.

Once your soul is well-rested, you have free will to decide how you want to incarnate next. You prepare your soul plan and after your guides approve it, then it is time for you to come back.

Earth is just a school and we keep coming and going like shooting stars. That is how quickly the process of life and death happens. Time does not matter. In the spirit world, time is of no significance—it is an Earthly concept. Therefore, one lifetime could feel like two seconds in the other plane, while on Earth, it may seem like days are slowly moving.

In the spirit realm, there is a lot of transparency. You can telepathically communicate with souls and you will instantly know what is happening. On Earth, we cannot read each other's thoughts but we can read energy, and energy does not lie.

YOU CREATE YOUR FUTURE

The present is so important because the truth is the future is not set in stone. Your future is up to you. We know who we are but we are still living in ignorance. If you are taking wrong actions, you are creating a future where you will have to repay that bad karma. Good actions lead to a better life, so focus on being a kind person and spreading positive energies wherever you go.

We believe that what we see is what is real, but life is so much more. There are sounds and vibrations we do not see or hear but we can feel. Love emits a light that you can see if you tune in to that energetic vibration. Most of our world is living from the first three chakras. Spiritual ascension begins in the Heart chakra. Once you feel love and compassion for humanity, you rise above and vibrate higher. Raise your vibe so that when you die your soul leaves from the Crown chakra.

DEATH TAKES IT ALL

You cannot hang on to your Earthly possessions. Detach yourself from them so that you can let it all go. Just live in the here and now. This moment is all.

The process of dying is interesting, and if you study it long enough, you will realize we never really die. The soul is eternal and immortal; only the body withers and falls away once it is old. You are already one with God when you die. You are dying at each moment. You are living and dying at the same time. It is not just 80 years of existence, but 80 years of death.

We don't belong to Earth; we belong to the Source. Earth is a hotel that is housing us. This planet is our school, and we must not spoil our school.

Remembering that we have limited time on this planet and that we are here to accomplish a mission will help you make the big choices in life. You have limited breaths, so you must not put things off for the future. Have the courage to follow your inner voice. This is the only way you will ever attain freedom in the afterlife.

You are a creator. You are here for a special reason. You can create your life the way you want it by affirming that into existence. It always starts now. Once you realize the power lies within you, deep in your heart, you start attracting abundance in your life.

Now, put yourself out there and live your soul's purpose!

Acknowledgments

I am immensely grateful to my parents, Capt. Manoj Gandhi and Manju Gandhi, for believing in my dreams and encouraging me to relentlessly pursue them until they come true. Thank you for your unconditional love and endless support, always.

I am indebted to my teachers, Joey Wargachuk, Joann Anderson Homen, Craig Davidson, and Chris 'Dub' Whittaker, who guided and supported me through the process of writing this book.

I am truly grateful to my close friends and relatives in India, Canada, and the rest of the world who helped me get to the finish line. You know who you are and I love you all.

Lastly, a big thank you to the entire team at Archway Publishing for their suggestions and patience as I perfected this manuscript.

Thank you, thank you, thank you!

Afterword

In Hinduism, the word *"Dharma"* denotes fulfilling one's duty and living as per divine law. It amuses me how big a synchronicity it is that my first book is dedicated to helping you find your life's mission and understand your soul's purpose when writing this book has been my soul's purpose for the longest time.

The knowledge and wisdom in this book were channelled from higher realms. My spirit guides instructed me to include certain topics and share my soul's learnings from past lives. You are now holding a book of ancient secrets and magical wisdom brought to life after connecting to planet Earth and the heavenly Source.

May this guidebook inspire you to find the light that lives within you deep inside.

Glossary

Atman

In Hinduism, *Atman* is the Sanskrit word for the soul, the innermost essence within each being. Atman, or the soul, cannot be destroyed; it has always existed and will continue to do so.

Akashic Records

The Hall of Akashic Records (or the Hall of Records/Hall of Journals) is a library of consciousness that is encoded in the non-physical plane of existence. It houses sacred books encrypted with detailed aspects of each Earthly life your soul has lived. Your thoughts, words, and actions are recorded daily in the Akashic Records under your soul name, and the collective story your soul is living is showcased karmically through these Records.

Aura

Every living being has an energy field surrounding its body which is its aura, reflected through colours and light. Positive, high vibrational souls have a brighter and lighter aura, and critical, low vibrational souls have a darker and heavier aura.

Brahma

In Hinduism, *Brahma* is the ultimate reality. It is the Sanskrit name for the creator God of the Hindu sacred triad including Vishnu, the preserver God, and Shiva, the destroyer God.

Conscious Mind
This is the objective or the rational mind that contains all the thoughts, memories, feelings, and desires in your awareness at any given moment. This is the thinking mind you use for everyday functioning.

Enlightenment
In Buddhism, enlightenment is the attainment of peace so profound that it is undeterred by desires or suffering.

Ego Identity
This is the self that positions itself separate from another self or the world.

Higher Self
This is the eternal and omnipotent self that is your real identity.

Kali Yuga
In Hinduism, this is the fourth and final cycle of the world that we are presently in. *Kali Yuga* is the age of darkness, sin, conflict, hypocrisy, doubt, and discord.

Karma
In Hinduism and Buddhism, karma is a Sanskrit word for actions generated by desire that cause the cycle of cause and effect.

Maya
In Hinduism, *maya* is a Sanskrit word for illusion, denoting the cosmic illusion that this Earthly realm is real.

Moksha
In Hinduism, *moksha* signifies freedom or liberation from the cycle of death and rebirth. Self-realization brings about *moksha*. This is the goal for each soul.

Mudra
In Hinduism and Buddhism, *Mudra* is a Sanskrit word for a symbolic gesture or pose denoting divine power.

Past Life
This is the previous life a soul led. A past life regression can help shed light on traumas or conflicts that are causing issues in the present life.

Real Self
See Higher Self.

Reincarnation
In the teachings of Hinduism, reincarnation is the process of the soul going through continual cycles of rebirth. In each lifetime, the soul enters a new human body in a different setting on Earth to learn life lessons and repay karma to soul mates.

Soul
See *Atman*.

Soul Mate
These are your fellow soul mates attending the same Earthly school as you. The relationship you share could be positive, negative, or neutral. Each soul mate is on its unique path, and you both may share good, bad, or neutral karma.

Spirit Guide
This is your guardian angel assigned to you at birth to protect, heal, and help you.

Spirit Realm
This is the heavenly realm where we come from and where we will return once this life ends.

Subconscious Mind

This is the part of the mind that stores habits, thoughts, and emotions that are not in the state of conscious awareness.

Telepathy

This is the ability to communicate with another mind by sending and receiving thought impulses.

Twin Souls

This is the other half of your soul. When a soul begins its journey, it is split into a male and female form. Both souls strive to reunite after paying their karmic debt to form the whole soul and attain enlightenment in this Universe.

Vibration

Each emotion emanates a vibration. Happy emotions give out a high vibration, and sad emotions give out a low vibration.

Recommended Reading

A Life After Death by Dr. S. Ralph Harlow
Autobiography of a Yogi by Paramahansa Yogananda
Born to Heal by Ruth Montgomery
Death and Its Mystery Before Death by Camille Flammarion
How to Know God by Deepak Chopra
Inspiration by Dr. Wayne W. Dyer
Life After Life by Raymond Moody Jr., M.D
Many Lives, Many Masters by Brian L. Weiss M.D
Many Mansions: The Edgar Cayce Story of Reincarnation by Gina Cerminara
Messages from the Masters by Brian L. Weiss M.D
Mystery of Life, Death and the Beyond by F. Rustomjee
No Mud, No Lotus by Thich Nhat Hanh
Only Love is Real by Brian L. Weiss M.D
Same Soul, Many Bodies by Brian L. Weiss M.D
Soul Healing Miracles by Dr. & Master Zhi Gang Sha
Synchrodestiny: Harnessing the Infinite Power of Coincidence to Create Miracles by Deepak Chopra
The Buddha and the Badass by Vishen Lakhiani
The Complete Ascension Manual – How to Achieve Ascension in This Lifetime by Joshua David Stone, Ph.D
The Afterlife Revealed: What the Dead are Telling Us About Their World by Stafford Betty
The Calling by Julia Mossbridge
The Greatest Secret by Rhonda Byrne

The Key to Living the Law of Attraction by Jack Canfield and D.D. Watkins
The Numerology Handbook by Tania Gabrielle
The Power of Now by Eckhart Tolle
The Toltec Art of Life and Death by Don Miguel Ruiz
Twenty Cases Suggestive of Reincarnation by Ian Stevenson, MD
You Can Heal Your Life by Louise Hay
You Will Survive After Death by Sherwood Eddy

Select Bibliography

Bhavnagri, Khorshed. *The Laws of the Spirit World. Jaico Publishing House*, 2010.

Bunker, Dusty. *Numerology, Astrology & Dreams. Whitford Press*, 1987.

Carroll Richardson, Tanya. "Soulmate: 12 Types Of Soul Mates & How To Recognize Them." *Mind Body Green Relationships*, 8 Dec. 2022, www.mindbodygreen.com/articles/types-of-soul-mates. Accessed 30 Dec. 2022.

DeMarco, Jolie. *High Vibe Crystal Healing. Llewellyn Publications*, 2019.

Dvorsky, George. "14 Interesting Examples of the Golden Ratio in Nature." *Mathnasium*, 24 Apr. 2017, www.mathnasium.com/blog/14-interesting-examples-of-the-golden-ratio-in-nature. Accessed 5 Oct. 2022.

Easwaran, Eknath. *The Bhagavat Gita. Nilgiri Press*, 2007.

Gunaratana, Bhante. *Mindfulness in Plain English. Wisdom Publications*, 2019.

How to Read Tarot. Adams Media, 2017.

Howe, Linda. *Healing Through the Akashic Records. Sounds True, Boulder Colorado*, 2014.

Hurst, Katherine. "Numerology Calculator: Your Life Path Number And Meaning."

TheLawofAttraction.Com, 11 Jan. 2019, thelawofattraction.com/life-path-number-challenges/. Accessed 3 Feb. 2021.

Kelly, Aliza. "Birth Charts 101: Understanding the Planets and Their Meanings." *Allure*, 4 Jul. 2021, www.allure.com/story/astrology-birth-chart-reading. Accessed 27 Jul. 2022.

Kelly, Aliza. "12 Zodiac Signs: Dates and Personality Traits of Each Star Sign." *Allure*, 2 Jan. 2023, www.allure.com/story/zodiac-sign-personality-traits-dates. Accessed 10 Jan. 2023.

Rawles, Bruce. "Sacred Geometry Introductory Tutorial." *The Geometry Code*, 22 Feb. 2010, www.geometrycode.com/sacred-geometry/. Accessed 27 Jul. 2022.

The Three Initiates. *The Kybalion: A Study of The Hermetic Philosophy of Ancient Egypt and Greece. Sunsight Press*, 2021.

Tripathi, Latika. *Don't Cry When I Die. Dhruv Publishing*, 2010.

"Hinduism: Basic Beliefs." *United Religions Initiative*, 1 Dec. 2018, www.uri.org/kids/world-religions/hindu-beliefs. Accessed 9 Sept. 2020.

"The Best Careers for Every Zodiac Sign." *Yahoo! Finance*, 23 Jan. 2022, finance.yahoo.com/news/best-careers-every-zodiac-sign-160800006.html. Accessed 27 Jul. 2022. "The Best Jobs for Your Astrological Sign." *ZipRecruiter*, 31 Mar. 2022, www.ziprecruiter.com/blog/the-best-jobs-for-your-astrological-sign/. Accessed 27 Jul. 2022.

About the Author

Shweta Gandhi earned a bachelor's with honours in journalism, a post-graduate diploma in print journalism, a master's degree in fashion journalism, and a certificate in digital strategy and marketing management. She's a Toronto-based journalist, writer, and editor. Her work has appeared in publications such as *CBC Life, Vogue India, ELLE India, Girlboss, Regarding Luxury,* and *Elixuer.* Gandhi has also worked as a digital copywriter for leading retail brands. Visit her online at svetarotreading. com and shwetagandhi.ca.

Notes

Printed in the United States
by Baker & Taylor Publisher Services